As

Needed

for

Pain

a memoir of addiction

As

Needed

for

Pain

DAN PERES

HARPER

An Imprint of HarperCollins*Publishers*

HarperCollins books may be purchased for educational, business, or sales
promotional use. For information, please email the Special Markets
Department at SPsales@harpercollins.com.

FIRST EDITION

Designed by Elina Cohen

Library of Congress Cataloging-in-Publication Data has been applied for.

ISBN 978-0-06-269346-4

20 21 22 23 24   LSC   10 9 8 7 6 5 4 3 2 1

TO OSCAR, SAM, AND JULIAN—

FOR SHOWING ME THE WAY

Contents

CONTENTS

EVERYTHING THAT I WRITE ABOUT in this book actually happened. (Sorry, Mom.) The events I describe are based on my memory and interpretation of some truly unforgettable—and regrettable—experiences and interactions. This is, however, *my* story, and as such, I have changed the names and identifying characteristics of many of the people mentioned—childhood friends, girlfriends, acquaintances, all of the doctors (except for my pediatrician), etc., as well as altering the exact location of several events. I have also changed the name of at least one business—Elegant Affairs. I did my best to stay true to chronology, but one or two minor things have been moved around to make for more linear story-telling. Lastly, I tried to be as accurate as possible with respect to the quantity and dosage of the pills I was taking—but as the pages you're about to read will illuminate, sometimes things got a little fuzzy.

As

Needed

for

Pain

PILLS

PILLS ROLL. FIRST THEY BOUNCE and then they roll.

Shape doesn't matter. Perfectly round. Oblong. Squares with rounded corners. Capsules. It may defy the laws of physics, but in the end they all roll. I've dropped more pills than the average person swallows in a year, and when they hit the floor, they scatter like roaches. And when they roll, they don't stop until they've reached the farthest, most undesirable destination imaginable. Deep under beds. Wedged beneath the floorboard. Hidden in plain sight in the low pile of wall-to-wall carpeting. And, as it turned out on one particular evening in early 2003, under the urinal in the bathroom at the Waldorf Astoria. Three of them, to be precise, which—on a bended, tuxedo-clad knee—I rescued, promptly put in my mouth, and swallowed.

It's not the first time I did something I'm not proud of while wearing a tuxedo.

There was the night I threw up in a garbage can in Times Square on my way home from a benefit performance of some Broadway show. I can't remember the name of the show, but I do remember a man with a ponytail and a leather vest clutching his date tightly by the arm as they walked past me on a crowded sidewalk. "Don't look," he told her. "Just keep moving."

Then there was the time I stole a bottle of Valium from the master bathroom medicine cabinet of my friend Ingrid's parents' Upper East Side duplex while everyone was downstairs toasting her thirtieth birthday. I didn't just take a few pills like any normal self-respecting degenerate might. No, I literally pocketed the whole bottle. Not just all of the contents of the bottle, but the actual bottle. They rattled like Tic Tacs in the breast pocket of my tux as I made my way past a multicolored Calder mobile and down the sweeping staircase to rejoin the party.

And there was the middle-of-the-night trip to the emergency room at St. Vincent's, where I conned an exhausted young doctor into giving me a prescription for thirty Vicodin after being repeatedly flashed in the waiting room by a woman in a pink paper gown.

I was in black tie for all of them. Dressed to impress—just as I was that night at the Waldorf Astoria in 2003. I was attending a gala fundraiser. Invitations to events like these were common, even if my attendance at them was infrequent. Sometimes Condé Nast, the publishing giant for which I'd been working as the editor in chief of *Details* for a few years by this point, would buy a table and I'd be asked to join. Other times, the evening would honor an executive or designer from a fashion company and the organizers would try to fill tables with editors, celebrities, and celebrity editors. I was, I assumed, a Plan B guest: fit to attend, but not first choice— like an alternate on an Olympic team.

And I was rarely invited with a plus-one, though I wouldn't have brought anyone had I been. As with just about everything else I did, I preferred to go to these functions alone. Plus-ones gave me anxiety. They slowed me down. They wanted to be treated like humans. They wanted to show up on time and be introduced to people and mingle and eat and stay for the performance. There was always a performance. Once, shortly before September 11, 2001, after she had been asking for months to join me at one of these, I finally agreed to bring my long-suffering, nightlife-loving girlfriend Caroline along. And of course she insisted on staying for the performance. I think it might have been Patti LaBelle. Or maybe it was Gladys Knight. Either way, Caroline wasn't interested in leaving when I was.

"Can we please just get out of here?" I pleaded halfway through the dinner. I was high—I was always high—but not nearly high enough for another hour and a half of small talk and rubber chicken.

"What is *wrong* with you?" she asked for the thousandth time in our relationship.

"I'm not here to have fun," I said. "This isn't fun for me. This is work."

"Work? We're at this amazing party with all of these incredible people and an R&B legend is about to perform," she said in the type of clipped loud whisper often reserved for public spats.

"All of a sudden Miss Indie Rock is dying to see the Queen of Soul?"

"Aretha Franklin is the Queen of Soul, asshole," she said.

"I knew I shouldn't have brought you," I shot back. "Plus, everyone is staring at your nipples."

"You're a dick," she said.

She was right. I was dick. A dick in a tux.

FROM THAT POINT ON, there were no more plus-ones. And so I went alone to the children's benefit at the Waldorf in early 2003, but not before doing something else I wasn't particularly proud of. Something that my fashion magazine colleagues would have frowned upon perhaps even more than my drug addiction.

I went to the tailor and let out my tuxedo.

Getting fat in fashion was never in fashion.

I wasn't what the editors of *Details* referred to as "sexy fat," either. This was actually a thing. We once published a story about the Tony Soprano Effect and how "heft had become hot." Guys like James Gandolfini and Julian Schnabel and Jack Nicholson. Guys who owned it and never bothered to suck it in. That wasn't me. I was more like Philip Seymour Hoffman's character, Scotty, in *Boogie Nights*, awkward and fleshy and testing the limits of my clothing in ways that made just about everybody uncomfortable. Nothing worse than bulges in all the wrong places. I was eating a lot.

There were meals and there were feedings.

Meals were food. Feedings were drugs. Both were vital and well planned. And I consumed both with gluttonous delight. As a rule, feedings generally preceded meals. Drugs kicked in faster on an empty stomach.

My diet alone should have been enough to kill me. I had developed a three-bagel-a-day habit. At 10:30 A.M., on my way to the office and around two hours after the day's first feeding of fifteen extra-strength Vicodin, I would pick up a toasted everything bagel with two eggs, bacon, and Swiss cheese.

"Don't forget to butter the bagel—both halves," I'd remind the guy behind the counter.

Once in my office—a small square room with giant windows overlooking the Empire State Building, framed *Details* covers lining the walls, an overstuffed beige love seat, and a round blond wood table that served as my desk—I'd open a couple of small to-go salt packets and dump them out onto the greasy foil that wrapped my morning delicacy, then dunk the sandwich, glistening and slick, into a mound of salt before each bite. As if everything bagels weren't already salty enough. I was going for maximum bloat.

Lunch usually happened at around two—a couple of hours after my midday feeding of fifteen Vicodin—and was generally either a smoked turkey, a Black Forest ham, or a tuna sandwich on a plain bagel with a bag of chips and a Diet Coke from the company cafeteria.

I usually didn't eat dinner until 8:30 or 9:00 P.M. I'd survive on Cool Ranch Doritos, Twizzlers, three or four Diet Cokes, and half a pack of Marlboro Mediums between my 4:00 P.M. opiate feeding (fifteen pills) and dinner—the only meal of the day that I ate before taking drugs.

The evening feeding—the final feeding of the day—was the most important. This was the high I fantasized about during all of the other highs. This was the highest high of the day. Daytime doses had become little more than maintenance—just enough of an energy boost to get me through the day without unraveling, like a cell phone with a dwindling battery that gets plugged in here and there during working hours, but doesn't get the charge it really needs until the end of the day. The evening feeding was the biggest of the day. I'd usually add two or three pills on top of the now standard fifteen. I wanted a more intense buzz at bedtime. And I needed it to sleep, like a child's threadbare blanket. Seventeen or eighteen Vicodin. Lights out.

But first, dinner.

"Phish Food?" the voice on the other end of the phone would ask. "One or two?"

The guys working the counter at the deli around the corner

from my apartment knew my voice and would rattle off my order even before I could. Smoked turkey on a plain bagel with sliced mozzarella and shaved lettuce. A pint of Ben and Jerry's Phish Food, a pack of cigarettes, and a Diet Coke, which I drank while the sandwich was being warmed in the microwave. I'd fill the empty bottle with a couple of inches of water and use it as an ashtray for the rest of the night. Sometimes, at around midnight, I'd have to add more water to the foul, sludgy mixture. The Ben and Jerry's would also get microwaved—to the consistency of a milkshake. I'd eat it mostly with a spoon while leaning against the kitchen counter, but wasn't opposed to drinking the bottom third right out of the responsibly sourced, eco-friendly container before crushing it in my hand like a triumphant frat boy after shotgunning a beer.

THE TUX WAS a little snug.

It was a last-minute trip to the tailor, but they agreed to turn the tuxedo around quickly for me because I made sure they knew I was the editor in chief of *Details*. Though I would never promise, the possibility of coverage in the magazine was enough to open many doors—and, as it turned out, seams. Entitlement suited me well, just as the lightweight Super 150 midnight-blue Armani tux had about fifteen pounds ago.

When I was in my early twenties and a junior reporter at *Women's Wear Daily*, I was sent to interview legendary *GQ* editor Art Cooper about the state of media. Hanging on the wall in his spacious midtown office was a print of a Slim Aarons photo of Gary Cooper, Clark Gable, Van Heflin, and Jimmy Stewart. It was called *The Four Kings of Hollywood*, and all four men were standing at a bar in Beverly Hills wearing tuxedoes.

"Look at the ease with which they carried themselves. The elegance," Cooper told me. "This photo should be a beacon for all men. Hollywood's true power brokers at the time." The following day, I actually tracked down Slim by phone and asked about purchasing a copy of the famous photo, but changed my mind when he told me how much it would cost. Still, I thought about it every time I put on a tux. When I finally got my own shortly after taking the job at *Details*, it felt like a rite of passage—another box I needed to check on my way to feeling like a grown-up. Power brokers owned tuxes.

BY THE TIME I arrived at the Waldorf that evening in early 2003, the cocktail hour had already ended and dinner was being served. I picked up the place card with my name written in calligraphy across the front and headed over to my table. I had a small wooden box in my apartment filled with these cards. The box was polished walnut and had a silver-colored metal plate with my bar mitzvah invitation engraved on it attached to the lid— a gift from my stepfather's aunt Gilda. She was one of half a dozen step-great-aunts whom I saw no more than once or twice a year on a Jewish holiday or some family function. These aunts were indistinguishable from one another, and while sweet, all seemed to smell like smoked fish and Bengay.

At first glance, the cards in the box all looked the same—white, rectangular, a blur of black ink scrawled on one side—as alike as my stepfather's aunts. But they weren't. Some were linen. Others stood like tents. Some came in tiny envelopes. There was calligraphy, of course, but printed versions, too—a mix of bold and italics. *Mr. Daniel Peres.* **Dan Peres.** *Daniel Peres, Details.* Keepsakes of the world I both loved and loved to hate. Reminders that I was there—that I'd been given a seat at the table. Like Steve Martin when he excitedly flipped through the phone book in *The Jerk*, I'd been given long-sought validation by these little cards. "I'm somebody now."

Card in hand, I took my seat at the large round table. The auction was about to begin. In addition to charging a fortune for tables at these fundraisers, organizers also asked companies to donate items that could be auctioned off in order to raise even more for the designated charity—in this case, kids with diabetes. I always made it a point to bid in these auctions, even though I never won. I knew I'd never win. I'd learned over the years that if I got my hand up when the auctioneer—usually a well-known news anchor—called for starting bids, that I could show interest and a willingness to contribute without actually getting stuck writing a check. These bids could climb into the tens of thousands of dollars. I figured bidding early was an impressive display of wealth and compassion. Maybe someone might think that I, too, was a power broker. I wasn't interested in winning two seats on the 50-yard line at a Giants game and a football signed by the team. Auction would start. Hand would go up. Bidding would go up. Hand would come down.

Pushing my name card—*Daniel Peres* handwritten on heavy stock—into the inside breast pocket of my tuxedo in preparation for what I hoped would be a successful faux bid, I discovered a tissue tucked in the bottom of the pocket with what felt like five pills wrapped inside. This rarely happened. I was usually fastidious about managing my supply and seldom left pills somewhere and forgot about them. But when it did happen, when I did find a few Vicodin hidden in the back of a drawer or buried in a pocket, it was like winning the lottery—like finding one last M&M in the crumpled package you're about to throw away.

I could hardly contain my excitement at the discovery of a mini-stash and excused myself to the bathroom to investigate. In I went, past the attendant over to the relative privacy of the urinals, which were unoccupied. I hastily pulled the tissue from my pocket, accidentally dropping some pills—three Vicodin bouncing away like the tiny bubbles in the champagne glasses on the tables just outside.

I popped the two pills that remained in the tissue into my mouth and swallowed them with a gag and a shiver before searching for the others, which had settled in close proximity of one another under the last white porcelain urinal in a bank of three.

The surface below a urinal—even a urinal in a five-star hotel—is the same thing as the urinal itself. Urine. Spit. Wiry lone pubes inexplicably left behind like abandoned socks on a dingy laundromat floor. And, in this case, three Vicodin forming a near-perfect isosceles triangle on the bespattered tile just to the right of the urinal.

Does the five-second rule count for piss-soaked drugs?

I'd like to say I hesitated. That I took a moment to weigh my options. That I considered walking away. Surely a grown man should know better. Particularly one in a tuxedo.

But then again, I've swallowed some truly unsavory things in pursuit of a high. Basic pocket lint was pretty standard. I once unknowingly took a swig from a beer bottle that had a cigarette floating in it to coax a small handful of pills down my throat.

Then there was the time I drank gasoline. A great big gulp. Of gasoline. Or it may have been diesel. It's hard to know, but I suspect the flavor profiles are pretty similar.

Caroline and I were in the Hamptons at the time. It was her idea. Her friends. I didn't want to be there. I hated the Hamptons. The only thing I hated more than the Hamptons were the people in the Hamptons and the way they referred to going to the Hamptons as "heading east for the weekend." I put that on par with asking someone where they went to college and being told "I went to school in New Haven."

Plus, I wasn't a huge fan of being in the sun or on a beach or taking my shirt off in public. And I wasn't interested in being around active people. They were always training for something. A *tri*. A *half*. A *whole*. More like a-hole, if you asked me. I was starting to dislike people, more and more—especially healthy, tan, active people.

Caroline wanted to water-ski, which of course annoyed me. To make matters worse, she insisted on having me ride along in the boat. As it turned out, I had to swim a few yards from the end of the dock to the idling boat, and I had eight OxyContin in the pocket of my bathing suit. My only option was to quickly shove them in my mouth as I dove in and then take a giant gulp of bay water in order to swallow them. A layer of gasoline must have settled on the water as the boat bobbed gently in neutral, its two outboard engines humming away. It was like drinking straight from the pump. My throat felt like it'd been shredded by a thousand razors. My stomach burned. I wanted to vomit, but I fought to keep the Oxys down. I tasted fuel for the rest of the weekend.

The bathroom attendant at the Waldorf also wore a tuxedo. He was unusually tall. NBA tall. His tux definitely would have come from a store specializing in clothing men with uncommon body types. Did he see me drop my pills? For a moment, I worried what this man, this towering stranger, might think of me.

The moment passed.

I knelt down as if I was tying my shoes and snatched up the three Vicodin from under the urinal. Everything smelled of piss. I walked over to one of the sinks, which the attendant had turned on for me, put the pills in my mouth, and leaned in to take a sip of water from the faucet. Down they went. The attendant handed me a paper towel. While wiping my mouth I caught a glimpse of myself in the mirror.

I quickly looked away.

BRUT

THE FIRST REAL POWER BROKER I ever saw wasn't wearing a tuxedo. He wasn't wearing anything. He was completely naked.

I was eight years old.

He was just standing there talking baseball with a couple of other guys as if it was no big deal. He wasn't crouching over or turned to the side or rushing to get his undies on like I did when I had to change in front of the other kids at camp. He didn't have a care in the world, except whether or not the Orioles were going to make it to the play-offs.

And if his nakedness wasn't enough to completely mesmerize me, he also cursed. A lot.

"Weaver doesn't know what the fuck he's doing," he said, rubbing his tanned belly. "And Murray needs to swing that bat a lot fucking harder if we're going to have a chance."

The locker room smelled the way men should smell—like Brut deodorant. The smell was always there, as much a part of the room as the long wooden benches that separated rows of polished oak lockers or the dark red carpeting, which according to a sign hanging above the towel hamper, you couldn't walk across wearing golf shoes. The big green Brut aerosol can stood tall on a silver tray next to a line of five sinks. Beside it were a bottle of mouth-wash and small Dixie cups, Pinaud Clubman aftershave, and a container of black combs floating in a mysterious blue liquid.

The naked guy was one of the early morning swimmers. They were in their late sixties and arrived at the Bonnie View Country Club in Pikesville—the small, predominantly Jewish suburb in Baltimore where I grew up—before eight A.M., when the pool was designated for laps. In they went, every morning, punching at the water like exhausted prizefighters as they slowly made their way down and back.

I was there to play tennis with my grandmother and would usually have a quick swim before she took me home. Because I was eight years old, it was no longer okay for her to take me into the women's locker room. This was a relief. Grandma's friends were already frightening enough when they were fully clothed. They were squeezers and pinchers and kissers. I'd stand there frozen as they swooped in, lipstick smeared across the teeth, for an unwanted smooch. This was the stuff of nightmares. I hardly needed to see their pendulous breasts ever again. For the better part of my childhood, I thought a woman's nipples were meant to line up with her belly button like some sort of an anatomical ellipsis across the stomach.

The men, however, paid no attention to me. I just stood there staring at their weathered dicks and droopy old-man asses and listening to them go on about overpaid ballplayers. These were the Pikesville power brokers. The first-generation hustlers who came from nothing, turning small businesses—retail, electronics, real estate—into millions. They wore white terry cloth polo shirts and ate salami sandwiches for lunch. They played cards all after-noon. And they seemed to always smoke cigars—a chewed-up nub of a Macanudo permanently stuck between their second and third fingers. It was there when they drove their Cadillacs and swung their nine irons. It was there when they walked through the club-house to meet their wives for drinks. And it was there in the naked guy's hand as he talked shop.

How did an eight-year-old boy become a man? Nothing seemed more mystifying. Even then I felt like there was a handbook that explained all the rules for boys and girls, men and women, and that everyone had been given one except me. But these guys had figured it out. They had earned great livings and bought winter homes in Miami Beach. They had earned the respect of their families and the community. They were men among men who knew who they were, who'd earned the right to stand naked and had the confidence to do it. I wanted what they had.

I liked this locker room. Being there made me feel like one of the guys. So much so, in fact, that before heading out to the pool that morning, I hit each armpit with a quick spray of Brut.

It burned for days.

TAWNY

"HERE'S A SLICK YOUNG MAN. Feeling lucky? Come on, give it a shot."

Despite the fact that there was no one else in the room, it took me a second to realize that the dealer was talking to me. No one had ever called me *slick*.

The makeshift casino was set up in the bar across from the Bonnie View Country Club's main dining room, which tonight was covered with hundreds of red and silver balloons for Stephanie Bernstein's bat mitzvah.

I wasn't much of a gambler at thirteen, but I was desperate to get my hands on one of those poker chips. I'd been practicing coin vanishes and was struggling to find something that I could conceal undetected in my right hand. The *Tarbell Course in Magic*, volume 1—a must-read for any aspiring magician—specifically said that when doing the Classic Palm, the hand should look "completely natural" and your fingers should be able to move freely without dropping the hidden coin. The poker chips appeared to be the perfect size for my hands, and I wasn't leaving the party without one.

We'd gathered at Temple Beth El earlier that day to watch as Stephanie read from the Torah and gave a sobbing speech about a grandfather whom she was certain was "smiling down on me from heaven."

Touching though it was, the real highlight of the morning had little to do with Stephanie and everything to do with the debut of her older sister Dara's brand-new nose. Nose jobs were as common in Pikesville as BMWs. It was as if Oprah burst into the high school cafeteria one day and walked around shouting, "You get a nose. And you get a nose. And you get a nose."

Oprah failed to mention that they'd all be getting the exact same nose. It seemed like every plastic surgeon sourced parts from the same aftermarket distributor. It didn't matter if the patient came in with a Streisand or a Streep—when they left, they had a Ski Jump. Every time. Without fail.

The Ski Jump ran narrow from the bridge to the tip, as if pinched, finally forming a small rounded button, which turned slightly upward. There wasn't an edge or bump in sight. Moms and daughters would sometimes go in together for a package deal. The absolute worst was when one of the boys had it done. While this was obviously a one-size-fits-all unisex nose, it looked especially fake on a guy's face.

I got very used to seeing Ski Jumps around Pikesville. They were as easy to spot as the bad toupees my grandfather took great pleasure in pointing out when he'd see one at the country club. "Take a look at that rug over there," he'd say. "Who the hell does he think he's fooling?"

It was bar mitzvah season in Pikesville—the nine months every year when each weekend saw another batch of gawky thirteen-year-olds ascend toward adulthood with some over-the-top celebration. We took summers off for sleepaway camp, naturally.

Pikesville was the Jewish ghetto of the Baltimore suburbs—if ghettos had houses with three-car garages. The parties were meticulously planned and seemed to cost as much as weddings. There were fights over venues and deejays and caterers. Decades-old friendships were put to the test. And God forbid you had two invites for the same night.

For us kids, it wasn't as big of a deal, but for the parents this was serious business . . . and they kept score. Who was invited where? How much did each couple eat and drink? And how big was the gift that was handed over—*Goodfellas* style—in an envelope on the night of the celebration?

The highlight of my own bar mitzvah party wasn't being hoisted up in a chair as the bandleader, a black man in his forties, sang "Hava Nagila," or even holding hands with Marci Feldman as we danced to the band's rendition of Michael Jackson's "Wanna Be Startin' Somethin'," though that was definitely a milestone. No, it was when I got home and tallied up the checks. I'd been given close to $10,000.

The gifts were mainly $100 to $200, except for one whopper—$1,500 from the Westons, a wealthy couple who were clients of my stepfather's law practice and lived in Maryland horse country about an hour away. "You should have invited more gentiles," my grandfather told me when I showed him their check.

The Westons stood out for another reason, too. Mr. Weston wore a tuxedo while all of the other men were wearing suits. And Mrs. Weston looked like Linda Evans from *Dynasty*, her shoulder-length frosted blond hair something of an anomaly amidst the sea of black curls that were fairly standard in Pikesville.

But there were always some surprises at these parties, particularly when it came to outfits. Jeremy Kleiner's dad once showed up wearing a cropped fur coat and clutching what can only be described as a clutch. Someone's stepmom once wore a silky jump-suit that was so formfitting that she became the talk of the party and was single-handedly responsible for introducing the term *camel toe* into the lexicon of an army of pubescent young men. For the most part, though, the moms kept it simple with sequins or chiffon and the dads wore dark suits.

The boys also wore suits and ties for the parties that called for "formal attire." The girls put on dresses and walked awkwardly in their first heels, like baby giraffes on the verge of tipping over. Their spangled dresses took away all the mystery about the size and shape of their breasts, something that generally required a fair amount of guesswork with their usual shirts and sweaters.

Boobs had become a major preoccupation. My best friend, Adam Gold, had actually touched a pair over the bra at my bar mitzvah party, which was also held in Bonnie View's grand dining room a few months earlier. I had a ten-piece band and a giant ice sculpture that spelled DANNY.

"They were definitely Bs," he told me. "But she could be a full C by next summer." I nodded knowingly.

The working theory within my group of friends was that the bigger the boobs, the more willing the girl was to fool around. This had mainly gone untested, but seemed to make sense. My voice hadn't even changed and I barely had any hair on my body, so what did I know?

As waiters cleared away the dinner plates, the deejay called Stephanie to the center of the dance floor, where her cake sat on a lone table. There were thirteen long white candles, each lit by a family member she invited up after thanking them for being a part of her life. There were more tears as she lit the final candle in honor of the dead grandfather.

And just like that, the cake was gone and the instantly recognizable opening licks of Kool & the Gang's "Celebration" blared from the speakers. The dance floor was flooded and I quickly retreated in search of Adam, who had left the table forty-five minutes earlier as the entrées were just being served.

"It's easy, slick. You just put one of these chips on a number and I spin the wheel. If the ball lands on your number—boom, you're a winner."

I had on the navy blue suit I wore at my own bar mitzvah—my first ever—and I liked that this guy kept calling me *slick*. I felt like James Bond.

"Yeah, okay," I said after scanning the bar for Adam. The dealer was wearing a white suit jacket and had on a black derby hat, which I discovered was plastic as I stepped closer. This room was much darker than the dining room and was virtually empty. The music was loud in the background.

There's a party going on right here.

The chips were a touch smaller than a Kennedy half-dollar, with a smooth face and ridged edges. Red, blue, and yellow stacks sat on the green felt-covered table just in front of where he was standing. He slid about a dozen of the red ones over to me and gave the wheel a spin.

A celebration to last throughout the year.

I scattered the chips around on the numbered squares in front of me without much thought. I held one back in my right hand, casually placing it in my pocket as the dealer dropped the small white ball onto the spinning wheel. It didn't matter that I didn't win.

There wasn't much privacy for me to take a closer look at my new prize. The dining room was a full-blown disco by this point and the bar was starting to fill up with the adults who weren't interested in sharing the dance floor with a bunch of newly minted teens.

I certainly wasn't about to expose the stolen chip in front of the dealer, so I ducked out. I couldn't go back into the ballroom.

There was absolutely no way I was going to show my friends. My obsession with magic wasn't going to do me any favors with these guys. I was already something of an outlier because I hadn't yet made out with a girl and I wasn't terribly athletic. Confessing a love of magic would have made me about as cool as Doug Henning. It would have been social suicide.

I knew just where to go.

I made my way down the main corridor. Portraits of the club's past presidents lined the walls, brass name plates fixed to the bottom of each gilded frame. Rosenblatt. Goldberg. Samuelson. Cohen. Cohen. Cohen. It was either a dynasty or proof that Cohen is the Smith of the Hebrews. Ask any Jewish man if he knows Steven Cohen, and he'll tell you he knows at least five.

By the time I walked into the men's locker room downstairs, the noise from the party was nothing more than a distant vibration. I found a row of switches on the wall and flipped a couple until the lights above the sinks twitched to life. Standing in front of the mirror, I took the poker chip from my pocket and got to work. The familiar smell of Brut hung in the air.

"Watch carefully as I place the coin in my hand," I said to an invisible audience. I lightly gripped the chip between the muscles in my right palm, holding it in place as I pretended to drop it into the other hand. "And just like that . . . Presto, it's gone," I said as I slowly opened the fingers of my left hand, revealing it was empty.

This type of "performance" had become routine for me. I would often spend hours practicing in my own basement—after school and on weekends—surrounded by magic books, coins, and decks of Bicycle playing cards. "Was this your card?" I'd say to no one as I dramatically turned over the ace of spades.

"Who are you talking to?" my mother would shout from upstairs.

"Just playing," I'd yell.

This night was different, though. I was wearing a suit like a professional magician would. I felt like a real performer—like David Copperfield in the autographed photo I had of him elegantly levitating a beautiful woman.

I idolized Copperfield. He was graceful and funny and he had great hair. He wasn't goofy like Doug Henning with his tie-dyed shirts and porn-star mustache. Copperfield was polished. Plus, I'd heard he was Jewish. I would often sit in my basement carefully studying the VHS recordings I'd made of his television specials, stopping, rewinding, and desperately trying to figure out how he walked through the Great Wall of China or made the Statue of Liberty disappear.

Magic was the perfect escape from reality, because in the end, that is exactly what it's designed to do—defy reality. When I was performing a card trick, I stood up straighter and spoke louder and more slowly. Magic gave people a reason to look at me without actually looking at me. Still, it didn't matter, as I rarely performed tricks for anyone other than myself.

"Watch carefully," I said, studying myself in the locker-room mirror as I held the poker chip at the tips of my fingers. That's when I heard the giggling. I quickly pocketed the red chip. Through the corner of my eye I saw someone dash out of the locker-room attendant's office and run out the door. The lights weren't on over there and I couldn't tell who it was. All I could see was that it was a girl and she was holding her shoes.

"What's going on out here?" asked Adam, emerging from the same small office. He walked over to the bank of sinks where I was standing, picked up the Scope mouthwash that was on the counter, and sipped some right out of the bottle. He swished it around in his mouth before spitting into one of the sinks.

"Who just booked it out of here?" I asked.

"That was Jodi. Don't tell anyone, but I totally just felt her tits," he said. "She took off her bra. She took it off. Holy shit!"

Adam was the cool kid from the *ABC Afterschool Special*. The one who was good looking and could charm his way in or out of anything. It was effortless for Adam. Girls tripped over themselves to get close to him. Everyone loved him. And now Jodi Weinstein had just let him play with her gigantic boobs. Some guys had all the luck.

"Who were you talking to out here?" he asked.

"No one," I said.

"We heard voices."

"All right," I said, "I'll tell you, but you have to swear you won't say anything."

"I swear."

"I was with Stephanie's cousin, Tawny. The older one from out of town. We were fooling around. I got to second."

Tawny? What was I thinking? Jewish people didn't name their daughters Tawny. I panicked, and it was the first thing that came to mind. I must have seen Whitesnake's "Here I Go Again" video a thousand times and was obsessed with Tawny Kitaen doing splits on the hood of a Jaguar.

"Nice," said Adam. I'm pretty sure he didn't believe me, but he never called me out.

"Jodi definitely had Ds," he said. "How about the cousin?"

I put my hands in my pockets and looked down for a moment at my shiny penny loafers as they kicked at something that wasn't there.

"Same," I said. "Ds are my favorite."

MAGNUM OPUS

BY SIXTEEN, WHILE I WAS desperately praying for my first hand job like some horny Make-A-Wish kid, Adam was fast becoming the Jewish Wilt Chamberlin. Having sex with him became something of a bucket-list achievement for Pikesville girls in the late eighties.

Meanwhile, everything I knew about sex came from porn. My friends and I traded pornos like baseball cards. Need it. Need it. Got it. I studied these movies like they were the Dead Sea Scrolls. I knew every scene. Every plotline. It turned out that a lot of job interviews led to sex right there on the desk. I couldn't wait to join the workforce.

Acquiring new pornography was one of the great challenges of my adolescence, right up there with braces, acne, and parallel parking. Pikesville was hardly a hedonists' playground. Looking for a new menorah? A lean corned beef on rye with a side of slaw? Pikesville was the spot.

There was only one place in Baltimore that I knew of where I was sure to find what I was searching for—the Block. The Block was actually a stretch of several blocks downtown on East Baltimore Street. This area was as close to a red-light district as we were going to get: strip clubs, X-rated movie theaters, peep shows, seedy bars, and sex shops. As a kid, when we would drive past Baltimore Street on the way to a restaurant somewhere near the harbor, I would crane my neck to look down the Block with the hope of seeing naked women. I never did, though I did see a man urinating in the street once.

One day, not long after I got my license, I decided to drive downtown to the best of one of Baltimore's two magic shops, Yogi Magic Mart. The shop had been around since the late 1930s, and going there was one of the few things that could excite me—even more than new porn. Yogi's was packed with illusions, props, books, and posters. I could have easily spent all day there; in fact I had on many occasions. This particular afternoon I was hoping to find a copy of a short manuscript by Paul Harris called *The Immaculate Connection*. It was a part of a series entitled New Stars of Magic and taught a trick where the magician linked together three playing cards with their centers torn out, like cardboard doughnuts. David Copperfield had performed it on his CBS special earlier in the year and I was desperate to learn the secret.

As I was walking back to my car with the Harris manuscript in a yellow plastic bag, it dawned on me that I wasn't far from the Block. There were always news reports about fights and shootings and drug activity on Baltimore Street, but how bad could it be in the middle of the day?

I'm not sure what I was expecting, but I definitely didn't count on seeing businessmen in suits and ties coming and going from nudie joints. These guys could have been my neighbors or my friends' dads or the guy from temple who handed out candy to the kids after services. It appeared that the search for new material was a lifelong pursuit.

I ducked into the first sex shop I came to. It smelled like sweat and bleach. It smelled the way I imagined a crime scene might smell. I tried to be discreet, but subtlety can be tough to pull off when you're waiting in line to pay for a copy of *Great Sexpectations* and it's in a box the size of a phone book.

IN TIME, THE MORE SEX my friends had, the more my virginity stood out. I was the one guy in a group of five friends who couldn't manage to close the deal. I was the guy the girls came to for advice. I was the guy they complained to and cried to. I was the guy they hugged before going off with the other guy. I was the sweet and lovable sidekick. I was Duckie from *Pretty in Pink*. I was Cameron from *Ferris Bueller's Day Off.* I was every character ever played by Anthony Michael Hall.

My chance for leading man status finally came in the fall of 1989, a few months into my freshman year at New York University. I had just turned eighteen.

I met Rachel Gordon the second week of school in the cafeteria at Rubin Hall on the corner of 10th Street and Fifth Avenue. We'd made eye contact a few times around the dorm but hadn't spoken. There was something exotic about Rachel. She had olive-colored skin, long black wavy hair, and the icy blue eyes of a Siberian husky. There was a calm about her that was completely foreign to me. She lacked the unbridled anxiety that the Jewish girls I'd grown up around seemed to ooze. Rachel was a hippie, albeit one from Beverly Hills.

"I'm Dan, by the way," I said, when I finally worked up the courage to say hello. I had been Danny my entire life, but switched to Dan on my first day at NYU. It seemed more grown up. Less virginal.

Like most relationships, this one started off with a lie. We were having dinner at Dojo on West 4th Street after dating for a couple of weeks when she asked me how I lost my virginity. She lost hers at sixteen on a ranch in Ojai to her high school boyfriend, the son of a famous television producer. She told me that he kept a macrobiotic diet, introduced her to yoga, and looked like a young Jackson Browne. Needless to say, my history of chronic masturbation and coin tricks couldn't compete with that.

I spun some tale about sleeping with my neighbor's older sister the previous summer when she was home from college. It was the plotline of a porno I'd seen once.

Rachel was the oldest of three sisters, who were referred to by nearly everyone who knew them as the Gordon Girls. They all attended a small, elite private school near Beverly Hills—which Rachel called the Academy—where they had to wear a uniform of pale blue pleated skirts and white polo shirts with the school logo embroidered on the chest. Like me, Rachel had been the editor of her high school newspaper. She was one of the smartest people I'd ever met, often speaking passionately in opposition of the impending Gulf War. Her parents were big Democratic fundraisers in California, and Rachel knew more about politics than most adults I'd known. I would sit across from her on the floor of my dorm room and listen as she railed against the president. She was the first non-family member I ever said "I love you" to.

As dorm rooms go, mine on the fourth floor of Rubin Hall was fairly typical. My roommate, Sean, was studying photography at NYU's Tisch School of the Arts. He'd grown up in Manhattan and spent most nights and weekends with his parents in his childhood home on Central Park West. I never understood why he even bothered to pay for housing, but I wasn't complaining. Our room was originally meant for three people, but it was just Sean and me—mainly me.

There were bunk beds and a single bed separated by Sean's desk along the left-hand wall. I slept on the bottom bunk, which was closest to the window overlooking 10th Street, and Sean had the single, which was closer to the bathroom. The top bunk sat empty except for a navy blue fitted sheet and a bunch of decorative pillows courtesy of Sean's mom. I'd tucked a spare blanket under the mattress of the top bunk, which, when pulled down, turned my bed into the type of fort my brother and I used to make when we were kids with sofa cushions and my mother's expensive white throws. Along the opposite wall were our dressers, a mini-fridge stocked with ginger ale and black film canisters, and my desk.

The night I lost my virginity, Rachel and I had been studying in my room. Had I known I was going to finally be having sex that night, I probably would have dimmed the lights and put on some music. I definitely would have put on a new pair of boxers instead of the old Hanes tighty-whities I was wearing.

But it all happened so quickly. After fooling around on my bed for a few minutes, Rachel asked me if I had a condom. I did. I'd nervously purchased them the week before along with some Twizzlers at a deli on University Place. I'd hidden the box in the back of my sock drawer. I was in such a hurry to get one that when I jumped out of bed I knocked my head on the frame of the upper bunk.

"Are you okay?" Rachel asked.

I was standing there rubbing my head with a pair of tighty-whities around my ankles.

"Yup," I said. "All good."

My dresser was flush against the room's heater, which had kicked on a few days earlier as it had finally started to feel like fall in the city. The side of the dresser was hot. When I pulled the condom out of the drawer, it was warm. Adam and the other guys

I grew up with were always talking about how they preferred lubricated condoms, so that's what I bought. The only problem was
that it wasn't clear to me which way the condom went on. Was the
lubrication for me or for her?

I stood there looking at Rachel's naked body a few feet away.
It felt like I had been waiting my whole life for this moment. I'd
fantasized about sex for years. I'd seen it done in videos at least a
hundred times—by professionals, no less. My training was complete.
I was, quite arguably, the most well-prepared virgin in history.

So I took a deep breath and put on the condom, still warm
from the room's heater. Confused, I put it on inside out. The instant that warm lubrication hit my skin I got light-headed. It felt
incredible—better than anything I'd ever felt. It felt so good, in
fact, that I came right there standing in front of my dresser, an
empty Trojan wrapper by my feet.

Unsure as to whether or not Rachel knew what was going on, I
kept my cool. I walked over to her and put myself inside. We had
sex for about thirty seconds before I started to go limp. I had no
choice but to fake an orgasm. I jerked and shivered and groaned,
just like the guys in the pornos. I'd like to think I gave a convincing
performance.

"Oops," I said. "Sorry about that. I just couldn't control myself."

"No, that was great," she said. Sweet, but a lie.

It didn't really matter, though. While anyone else would have
viewed this experience as a disaster, to me it was a victory. It was
a rite of passage. I was no longer a virgin. I had finally caught up
to my friends. The next day, I ditched the remaining condoms that
were in the small box in my sock drawer. I was worried that the
heat had somehow damaged them. Plus, I couldn't afford another
lubrication mishap, no matter how good it felt. This time I went

to Rite Aid on Sixth Avenue to buy new ones, certain that they'd have a wider selection than the corner deli.

As a rule, buying condoms should be done quickly and with as few witnesses as possible. But I lingered. The selection was overwhelming and I was clueless. It must have showed.

"Can I help you find something?" the store clerk asked as he passed by where I was standing for the second time.

My first order of business was to let this guy know in no uncertain terms that he wasn't dealing with some dumb virgin.

"Yeah, I usually use these lubricated Trojans," I said, pointing at the blue box on the shelf, "and I like them a lot, but I'm looking to change it up."

"Okay, well, there's a lot here," he said. "There's ribbed and there's these without the lube. And I really like the lambskin. Have you tried those?"

"No," I said. "Not yet. Heard good things, though."

This should have been an extremely awkward conversation. This wasn't like buying new sneakers and having the salesman recommend a pair of Nike's. This was the dude stocking the shelf behind me with Dr. Scholl's shoe inserts telling me what he prefers while having sex. It should have been weird, but I was surprisingly into it. We were just two non-virgins talking shop.

"Oh, and Trojan just introduced these," he said, handing me a black box. It said MAGNUM in big gold letters across the front. Underneath, it read, "Large Size Condoms."

Now what guy didn't want to buy these? You didn't hide this box in the sock drawer, that's for sure. No way. You kept this right on the nightstand like a trophy. It doesn't make a difference how many times a man is told "size doesn't matter," it sure as hell matters to him. It mattered to me.

But was I a MAGNUM man?

I got the definitive answer to that question months later when I went to visit my brother at Cornell. It was his senior year and Jeff wanted me to experience one of his legendary fraternity parties before graduating. I had met his college friends over the years, but this was the first time that I was actually going to hang out with them.

The party was held on the ground floor of the large white fraternity house on Cornell's scenic Ithaca campus. It was nothing like NYU parties, which were confined to considerably smaller venues. I stayed close to Jeff all night. We drank tons of beer and danced with his girlfriend and her friends. Afterward we ate pizza from a food truck before passing out in his room in the fraternity house.

The following morning I was standing in the house's open, locker-room-style shower, hung over and trying not to vomit as hot water was beating down on me. From behind me I heard one of Jeff's fraternity brothers calling my name.

"Yo, Dan," he said. "Turn around."

I didn't move.

"Hey, little bro," he continued. "Come on. Let's have a look. Let's see if you're hung like big brother. Does it run in the family?"

I pretended not to hear him. I moved closer to the wall in front of me. He walked up to me and pulled me by my shoulder, turning me around.

"Nope," he said, laughing, and walked away.

I turned back around and leaned my forehead against the tiled wall in front of me as water pounded down on my back. I wanted to disappear, but the *Tarbell Course in Magic* hadn't covered that.

THE CARTWHEEL

I KNEW THIS GUY IN college who got a tattoo of a Grateful Dead dancing bear on his forearm just so he might have a better chance of sleeping with a sexy Deadhead in our English lit class.

"It's like Tom Cruise in *Risky Business*, man," Henry told me when I questioned his sanity. "I said, 'What the fuck.'"

Maybe he was vaguely familiar with some of the band's more mainstream stuff, but he was hardly a Grateful Dead fan. He was more of a flannel-wearing Pearl Jam guy, but he had fallen hard for Amanda, who rarely wore a bra and spent summers following Jerry Garcia and the guys around the country. So he went for it. The tattoo ended up looking more like an Ewok than anything else, and when the semester was over I heard that Amanda was sleeping with our lit professor. Henry later took to telling people who asked about the tattoo that he was a die-hard *Star Wars* fan and that he loved the quiet strength and intense loyalty of the tiny teddy-bear-like creatures from the forest moon of Endor. I'm pretty sure that didn't help get him laid, either.

I know guys who have done some seriously dumb shit over the years in an attempt to impress women. "What the fuck" decision-making has led to more misguided mohawks, piercings, fedoras, bottle service, and leather pants than anything else, to say nothing of the purchase of countless Ducatis. We've spent ages catcalling and serenading and bulking up and trimming down and putting ourselves in the most unnatural situations. Like the time in high school when I tried out for a production of *Our Town* in order to get the attention of Becky Turner, a stunning blonde who was cast as Emily Webb. I tried out for the role of George Gibbs, the male lead and Emily's love interest. My voice quivered all the way through the audition. I had a tough time focusing on the memorized passage about my love for Emily as I was delivering it not to Becky Turner, as I had hoped, but to a pimply sophomore named Stefan who was there to help build the sets. Staring longingly into Stefan's eyes while sharing an imaginary ice cream soda in Grover's Corners was not what I had in mind when I signed up. I didn't get the part, or any part for that matter. Instead, I was asked to be the assistant to the show's faculty director, Mrs. Carr. I accepted. This was the theatrical equivalent of being a water boy. Still, it put me in close proximity to Becky, who went to an all-girls Episcopal school in what my grandfather referred to as the "goyisha part of town" and looked every bit as innocent as the Virgin Mary herself.

I soon learned, however, that she was far from a saint. One day before rehearsal, I walked into the dressing room and saw her making out with Danny Garrison, who played George and also got to kiss her onstage during every performance. Because I was always with Mrs. Carr, taking down notes on stage direction and lighting, I was viewed as the teacher's pet and something of a narc. Once when I went outside behind the theater to round up the cast for a meeting, everyone—including Becky—quickly stubbed out their cigarettes and scurried.

Sadly, I failed to make an impression on Becky. Mrs. Carr, on the other hand, was definitely a fan. I was presented that year's drama award at a special schoolwide assembly for my exemplary work as director's assistant. It's the only trophy that I ever won—except for those participation awards given to the entire Little League team when I was ten and eleven.

Hands down, though, my single biggest "what the fuck" moment would have to be the cartwheel.

In 1995, not long before the cartwheel, I had just been promoted to what was described to me rather enviably on more than one occasion as "the best job in New York." I was the editor of the Eye page at *Women's Wear Daily*, the fashion-industry trade journal whose influence reached far beyond the cluttered showrooms of Seventh Avenue. *WWD* was the ultimate influencer for an audience of cultural influencers. It was a must-read—the definitive word on style, celebrity, and taste. Whether you were a designer, an artist, a chef, an author, or a Park Avenue socialite, coverage in *WWD* had the ability to anoint stars and make careers. It could also end them just as swiftly. I was in charge of the Eye, which showcased the paper's sharp-witted party coverage and celebrity profiles. It was my first taste of the power and access that comes with some jobs in journalism, and I liked it. It was a highly coveted position and one that I almost didn't get.

Like many businesses in New York back then, *WWD*'s parent company, Fairchild Publications, drug-tested prospective employees. After graduating from NYU, I spent months sending résumés to just about every major media outlet—newspapers, magazines, television stations. Aware of the possibility that I might eventually have to pee in a cup, I completely stopped smoking pot, which had become a daily activity since the beginning of my final semester. After a few months, with nothing in front of me except a stack of rejection letters from places like the *New York Times*, ABC News, the *Wall Street Journal*, and even *Details* magazine, I decided it was time for a much-needed bong hit. No sooner had I exhaled than the phone rang and I was asked to come in the following day to meet about a position at Fairchild's menswear trade newspaper called the *Daily News Record*, or *DNR*.

"Relax. Just start drinking tons of water right now," Adam told me after I made a panicked call to him in Baltimore. "You haven't even met them yet. They're not going to give you a drug test at the interview."

Everything always seemed to just work out for Adam. Not for me. I stayed up half the night thinking of a way to dodge a drug test that I wasn't even sure I was going to be asked to take. It was the most time I'd ever put into preparing for a test in my life.

I devised what I thought was an ingenious plan.

I showed up for my interview the next day lugging a duffel bag that I'd loaded with dirty laundry to make sure it looked heavy. After meeting with a few people over the course of an hour, I was offered a job as *DNR*'s knitwear editor.

"We just need for you to take a drug test before we can make it official," the paper's editor in chief told me.

"No problem. Unfortunately, I'm leaving from here to travel down to visit with my family in Baltimore for the week," I told him, motioning to the overstuffed duffel bag resting on the floor by my feet. "Happy to take that test just as soon as I return."

It worked. The following week I passed my drug test and started my career in journalism. Writing about men's sweaters was not exactly what I had in mind when I'd envisioned my life as a reporter. I always dreamed of becoming a war correspondent like David Halberstam or bringing down the president like Woodward and Bernstein. Never did I imagine I'd be writing about chunky cable knits, shawl-collar cardigans, or the benefits of layering with sweater vests. But I was grateful to finally have a job and embraced my beat. In no time, I was quite comfortable discussing the nuanced differences between merino, angora, cashmere, and mohair—by far the itchiest of the lot, particularly if it was sourced from older goats. The younger the goat, the softer the mohair. I'm certain Woodward and Bernstein didn't know that.

Growing up, I never gave much thought to my wardrobe. My only requirement was that my clothes had pockets to accommodate the vintage Walking Liberty half-dollars that I liked to carry around in case I wanted to practice some coin tricks. Even as a teenager, when my friends were rocking nylon parachute pants or whatever else they scored from Merry-Go-Round in the mall, I was rather indifferent to fashion. Every now and then I would steal something from my brother's dresser that I'd seen him wear earlier in the week, but his stuff never looked as good on me. Needless to say, my newfound appreciation for fashion took some by surprise.

When I was at home in Baltimore for the weekend shortly after taking the job at *DNR*, my mother walked into the kitchen wearing a new red sweater. "Oh, chenille," I said. "Love it."

She tilted her head to the side and looked at me lovingly for a moment before sitting down beside me at the white Formica kitchen table. "Honey, I want to talk to you," she said. "I want you to know how much I love you, and that if there's ever anything you want to tell me, that I'll be open-minded and supportive."

"Come on, Mom," I said with a sigh. "I'm not gay."

"Okay, baby," she said, gently patting my knee as if to put me at ease. "I'm just saying. There haven't been too many girlfriends, and, you know, you were never really interested in sports. And there's the magic. I just want you to know that it's okay with me if you are. You can tell me anything."

What I should have told her was that chenille was very "last year" and a bit passé, but that would have sounded, well, a little gay.

"That's great, Mom," I said. "Thanks."

I think she was disappointed.

In the end, my tenure as *DNR*'s knitwear editor was short-lived. A junior position on the Eye page at *WWD* opened up, and Fairchild's powerful editorial director, Patrick McCarthy, asked if I was interested. I took the job.

Working on the Eye page required that I attend parties, sometimes two or three a night, and then show up at the office the following morning to write copy and edit the pictures that were taken by the photographer who was assigned to accompany me. It was an unusual profession for a homebody, but I dove in. I had always enjoyed talking to strangers, and I absolutely loved talking to famous strangers.

When I was a high school senior, my mother took me to New York so we could tour NYU. Walking through Washington Square Park, we saw lots of lights and cameras and I spotted Rob Reiner standing on the sidewalk. I marched right up to him, introduced myself, and told him I was a fan and that I was considering going to college there. He shook my hand and wished me well. The following year, when I saw *When Harry Met Sally* and realized that's what they'd been filming that day, I felt an odd sense of accomplishment, as if I'd somehow had a hand in making the movie.

Getting people to talk about themselves was always far more interesting to me than talking about myself. Standing there with my reporter's notebook in hand at the edge of a red carpet or backstage at a fashion show or at the opening night gala of the New York City Ballet or Metropolitan Opera, I had confidence. People—celebrities, even—wanted to talk to me. They sought me out. It was like walking into a world of magic, like the one I'd created in my basement years earlier.

Women's Wear Daily's Eye page was a favorite of the company's legendary and mischievous publisher, John Fairchild. Mr. Fairchild, as everyone called him, loved to stir the pot and poke fun at fashion designers and socialites, many of them his friends. He delighted in feeding me scoops about who had been dining with whom at La Grenouille or who had a shitty seat on the Concorde, as if there were such a thing.

One day I was called over to Mr. Fairchild's desk—he sat out in the newsroom of the paper's vast 34th Street offices—after he returned from lunch.

"I've got a good one for you," he told me, his voice high-pitched and gleeful. "Oscar de la Renta was like a rooster in the henhouse today at lunch, as he dined surrounded by the grande dames of society."

Mr. Fairchild then proceeded to rattle off the names of the women who had lunched with de la Renta. I knew all of them except one.

"Sorry," I said. "Can you please spell that last one?"

You would have thought that I had leaned in and kissed him on the mouth. Everyone within earshot looked up at me in horror. Patrick McCarthy, who was standing next to me as I took down my notes, just slowly shook his head and told me to go back to my desk. He made his way over a few minutes later.

"Did you just ask John Fairchild to spell something for you?" he asked. "You don't ask the head of this company to spell a name. He's not some debutante you're interviewing at a party. What's wrong with you?

"New rule," he continued. "If Mr. Fairchild mentions someone to you and you're not sure who they are, pretend you know who they are, for Christ's sake, and then ask me later."

It was a good tip. Still, the best piece of advice Patrick ever gave me was never to forget why I was being invited to all of those fancy parties in the first place. He cautioned me when I first took the job to always remember that it was *Women's Wear Daily* they wanted at the party, not me.

"Don't make the same mistake I've seen others in this role make over the years," he said. "You are being invited because people want to see their picture in the paper. Be careful. Sure, you may become friendly with some of them, but by and large, these people are not your friends."

This was a mistake I wasn't likely to make. Making friends had never been my strength. When I was a boy, it was challenging for my mother to throw birthday parties for me. She would always have to include some of my brother Jeff's friends just to make the party minimum size of eight players at the bowling alley. Jeff collected friends. He had school friends and camp friends and lacrosse friends and college friends. He went away on "guys' weekends" and organized bachelor parties. He had inside jokes and nicknames.

I did have some friends, of course, but I wasn't very good at holding on to them. I was the kid who always left the sleepover before we went to sleep. I was the kid who always got hurt when we were playing touch football. I was the kid who never wanted to take his shirt off at the pool party. I joined a fraternity at NYU because that's what Jeff had done at Cornell, but I wasn't really a fraternity kind of guy in the end, and by junior year I didn't show up all that much.

By the time I was named senior editor of the Eye page in spring of 1995, my friends—as had been the case throughout most of my childhood—were Adam's friends. In fact, on the night of the cartwheel, I had plans to meet Adam and some of his college buddies after covering a party at Joan Rivers's palatial Upper East Side apartment. Adam had recently moved to New York to start work at a small graphic design firm with an office in the Flatiron Building.

Adam was waiting for me outside of Brother's BBQ on West Houston Street. "Tanner is running late," he told me. "He wants us to meet him in the lobby of his office. He has to go to a going-away party for someone from work and he wants us to come with him."

Tanner was Evan Tannenbaum, Adam's roommate from Connecticut College. He worked as an account executive at Saatchi & Saatchi on Hudson Street, a few blocks from the restaurant. I had gotten to know Tanner pretty well over the years. He was a short Long Island Jew who worked out five days a week and almost always wore a faded blue Mets hat. I had joined a gym with Adam and Tanner a few months earlier. I'd gone once.

There were three attractive young women with Tanner when he stepped out of the elevator into the Saatchi & Saatchi Building's vast marble lobby. They were all laughing. Tanner's height and thinning hair—hence the baseball hat—never seemed to negatively impact his luck with women. He was funny. When we would all go out, Tanner would always have some woman he'd just met giggling and genuinely interested in him.

He introduced us to his three attractive coworkers. I had always struggled to stand out when standing next to Adam. The fact that I had just been hanging out with Joan Rivers and a bunch of rich women with beauty parlor hairdos and nubby tweed Chanel suits was hardly going to make an impression. Plus, Tanner told them my name was Danny, which always made me feel like a six-year-old on a Big Wheel. Determined to get them to notice me, I decided it was time for a "what the fuck" moment.

So here I was, a twenty-four-year-old man wearing a navy blue Donna Karan suit standing in the art-filled lobby of the Saatchi

& Saatchi Building in lower Manhattan, with an overwhelming desire to call attention to myself.

So, as if possessed by some demon gymnast, I suddenly—and rather unexpectedly—did a cartwheel.

Tanner had just finished telling Adam and me that one of the young women, Phoebe, had recently been promoted to senior art director.

"Congrats," I said. "That's impressive. But can you do this?"

I raised my arms over my head like a circus performer about to execute his final death-defying routine. I took a few steps forward, more of a skip than a walk, and I went for it. My left hand hit the floor first as I sprung off with my feet hoping momentum and gravity would do the rest.

It bears noting that I had never been in great shape. I was skinny-fat—doughy in some areas and rail-thin in others—and had been since puberty. My arms, like my legs, were underdeveloped, to say the least. It's also worth pointing out that I had never done a cartwheel before in my life, though I'd seen Chris Farley do it a bunch of times on *SNL*—and I was definitely in better shape than he was. Still, how I expected my twig of a left arm to support the weight of my entire body was beyond me. Needless to say, I didn't stick the landing. I came crashing down on the marble floor like . . . well, like a grown man trying to do a cartwheel for the first time.

"Ouch," said Phoebe. "Are you okay?"

I wasn't, but I hopped up and laughed it off. I was embarrassed, but a bruised ego was the least of my problems. I went limping off to Tanner's friend's going-away party trying not to let anyone know how badly I'd hurt myself.

The following morning, I could barely make it from my bed into the bathroom. My back was killing me and I couldn't stand up straight. I took some Advil and a hot shower and tried to make it into the office to write about Joan Rivers's party for *WWD*. I was a few blocks away from the subway when I decided to turn back and go home.

"I'm going to get you in to see an orthopedist," my doctor told me when I called his office and explained it was an emergency. "It may not be until Monday, but I'm going to send you for an MRI now just to get it out of the way. In the meantime, no more cartwheels for a while."

On Monday morning, I took a taxi from my apartment in the Village to the orthopedist's office on Lexington Avenue and 63rd Street. I was lying down in the back seat for the entire ride.

"Do you lead a particularly sedentary life?" Dr. Portnoy asked as he studied the MRI report. "It looks like you did a number on your lower back."

I had indeed. There was a ruptured disc at the L5/S1 level of my spine, he explained.

"We can wait and see if the pain dies down and then try some physical therapy," he told me, "but I suspect you're going to need surgery."

He sent me home with a prescription for thirty Vicodin, told me to take one to two every four hours and stay in bed for the next couple of days. I scheduled an appointment to see him again later that week.

The Vicodin helped ease the pain immediately. I was still hunched over a bit and limped when I walked, but I was able to move around. After a few days, I went back to work. When I saw the doctor that Thursday, he said I could try therapy if I was willing, but that I still needed to wait a week or two to see if the pain died down some more.

For some reason, I woke up the following morning in agony. My back was hurting more than it had the day after the cartwheel. I took a Vicodin and waited for relief. When it still didn't come an hour later, I took another pill and eventually fell asleep. When I woke up after a half hour, I was miserable. I couldn't stand. I hobbled to the living room, took two more Vicodin, and put on the television. Soon I was feeling no pain. My whole body was warm and relaxed. I felt like I'd been wrapped in an electric blanket.

An unfamiliar level of comfort and calm came over me. This was a high that I had never felt—the same high I imagined my brother experienced when he scored the winning goal in a lacrosse game or that Adam felt when he had a threesome his junior year in college. This was the way I'd always wanted to feel.

A week later, my back still in agony and unable to walk without sharp pain shooting down my left leg, I had the first of two surgeries at New York's Hospital for Special Surgery to repair a ruptured disc. The operations were three weeks apart, and after each, I was prescribed a large bottle of Vicodin. Other than that one time before surgery—despite how great the high felt—I took the medication as prescribed. *One to two tablets every four hours, as needed for pain.*

Several weeks after the second surgery, as the pain gradually subsided, I stopped taking the pills every four hours. I took one or two a day to help me get through work, until I eventually didn't need them anymore. One morning before work, I reached for the bottle before stopping myself. I left for the WWD offices without needing—or taking—any Vicodin.

That evening when I was getting ready for bed, I saw the bottle sitting on the nightstand. I grabbed it and walked into the bathroom to put it in the medicine cabinet. I was about to close the cabinet when I thought, *Maybe I'll just take two to help me relax.* I opened the prescription bottle and shook two pills out into my left palm. I studied them for a moment before giving the bottle another shake.

What the fuck . . . I'll take four.

UNRAVELING, PART 1

I'VE TRASHED TWO HOTEL ROOMS in my life.

Nothing epic enough to move the needle on the Keith Richards/ Johnny Depp scale of hotel-room destruction, but for a quiet kid from Pikesville who spent his formative years alone in the basement practicing card sleights, they definitely merit honorable mention.

The first time it happened was in Hartford, Connecticut, in the fall of 1995. I was twenty-three and had been a reporter at *Women's Wear Daily* and *W* magazine for a little over a year. It was my first-ever business trip and the first time I'd spent the night alone in a hotel—in this case, a twenty-story Sheraton in the center of the city. It was the kind of place that had individually wrapped plastic cups stacked on the dresser and a rubber mat suctioned to the center of the bathtub to keep you from slipping. I had a standard room with a queen-size bed on the same floor as the pool—which made the hallway humid and smellier than the average Sheraton hallway.

It should have been one of the greatest nights of my life, and for a while, at least, it was.

I was in Hartford to meet David Copperfield. He was performing at the Civic Center there, and I had somehow managed to convince my boss that we should do a story on Copperfield for *W* magazine timed to the release of a book he was publishing called *Tales of the Impossible*. It was a collection of original stories written by writers like Ray Bradbury and Joyce Carol Oates about the power of magic, which, of course, was of zero interest to *W*'s rarefied audience. No, the story got the green light thanks to Claudia Schiffer. At the time, Copperfield was engaged to the German supermodel, who was at the height of her career and a regular on *W*'s glossy oversize covers.

"If this article is about magic, you're in trouble," my boss, Patrick McCarthy, told me from behind his large wooden desk in the 34th Street newsroom of *WWD*. "I'm not kidding. Remember, I know how you feel about magic," he added, with a judgmental smirk.

I had foolishly outed myself as a magic lover a few months earlier when I made a coin vanish and then reappear in the ear of the young daughter of an executive assistant who was visiting her mom at the office. Though she giggled and begged me to do it again, not everyone shared her enthusiasm.

"Did you just do magic?" Patrick asked, in the same incredulous and mildly offended manner that one might ask, *Did you just fart?*

"I have an idea," he continued. "How about you go back to your desk and make your copy for tomorrow's paper appear on time? That would be a great trick."

It turned out that magic tricks were about as fashionable in the fashion world as wearing a clip-on tie.

"Yeah, yeah. No magic. Got it," I promised after Patrick reluctantly said yes to the Copperfield interview.

I didn't care. This wasn't about the article for me. This was much bigger. This was bucket-list stuff. I was finally going to meet my childhood hero. And not just some quickie handshake and awkward photo backstage, the kind Copperfield did after performances for VIP ticket holders. This, at least in my eyes, was going to be a conversation—my chance to sit across from the man who, along with Adam and my brother, Jeff, had been a north star to me during my childhood.

David Copperfield had always been there for me when I needed to escape. I was nine when I saw his first CBS special. Every year after, fall couldn't come soon enough for me as I waited for his annual television broadcast—my Super Bowl. He gave me an alternative to the celebrated male archetype of suburban Baltimore. He didn't carry a lacrosse stick or wear corduroys with tiny whales on them. He was a quirky Jewish guy who did magic. What more could I ask for? He also always seemed to get the girl—definitive proof that magic wasn't nearly as much of a virginity protector as that other eighties basement pursuit, Dungeons & Dragons. Copperfield had the most beautiful assistants in his shows, who were constantly under his spell and dancing around with him, and he was always laughing and flirting with celebrity guests like Cindy Williams and Bernadette Peters. He gave me hope.

And of course he gave me magic.

I sat in my basement and watched in awe as he walked through the Great Wall of China and vanished a seventy-ton Orient Express railway car and levitated over the Grand Canyon. His television specials became the highlight reel of my youth. They were always recorded in front of a live audience, and when he spoke to the crowd—when he spoke directly to the camera—I felt like he was speaking directly to me. Few people spoke directly to me.

Now, on a rainy night in Hartford, Connecticut, David Copperfield actually was going to speak directly to me. I'd been taking a few Vicodin a week since my surgeries, mainly to help me zone out at night, but didn't bother bringing any with me on this evening as I wanted to be as clearheaded as possible for our conversation. I knew it was going to be memorable and that the cassette recording of our interview would no doubt become a cherished possession. I figured I'd keep it alongside the copy of *The World's Greatest Magic* that I bought at the Yogi Magic Mart when I was twelve years old and had been signed by Copperfield.

It was like I was twelve all over again when he appeared on-stage at the Hartford Civic Center. The theater went dark and a series of small spotlights danced around an antique elevator that was slowly being lowered toward the stage, stopping a few feet from the ground. The doors opened and the thin material on the other three sides retracted to expose a wrought-iron frame that allowed the audience to see right through to the back of the stage. It was completely empty. The doors closed and the material on the sides slid back into place. Suddenly the doors were open again and there he was. I had goose bumps.

Copperfield was taller in real life than I thought he would be. He wore a neatly pressed white button-down shirt and a pair of high-waisted black jeans, and his hair was big on top and long in the back—the Jewish mullet. Jerry Seinfeld and Ben Stiller had similar hairdos around that time, which led me to believe that all male Jewish celebrities in the mid-nineties were seeing the same hairdresser.

My seat, which had been arranged through Copperfield's press team, was dead center, ten rows back. The best—and to me, the only—seat in the house. There was nowhere else in the world I would have wanted to be. I watched in mouth-agape wonderment as he elegantly passed through a giant fan and vanished random audience members only to make them reappear moments later on the other side of the stage. My eyes filled with tears at the end of the show when he talked about how much he always dreamed about seeing it snow when he was a young boy and then made it snow throughout the entire arena.

The interview was held backstage after the show in a small room that was empty except for two large leather club chairs facing each other—about three feet apart—and a narrow table off to the side with a few bottles of water. I was more excited than nervous. Because of my job as the Eye editor of *WWD* and *W*, I was interacting with celebrities all the time and never seemed to get nervous. In fact, I was very much at ease around famous people. I felt a level of comfort with celebrities that I never managed to feel as a boy around my childhood friends. Movie stars and fashion designers didn't know that I went to college a virgin or that I got so homesick at camp that I had to go to the nurse. They had no clue that I was the last picked for a pickup game of basketball or that I refused to take my shirt off when it was decided that my team would be "skins." My team was always "skins."

So I generally didn't get weird in front of celebrities. Most of the time, anyway.

Wow! David Copperfield has freakishly long fingers.

That was my first thought the moment I met my hero. He walked into the room and introduced himself. I was finally face-to-face with him, shaking hands with the man I'd idolized for most of my life, and all I could think was that he had unbelievably long fingers—like E.T. long. I'm pretty sure I held on to his hand a few beats longer than is customary for the average handshake. I've heard that some professional athletes are born with larger lungs, which gives them superhuman ability. Like a form of genetic superiority. Maybe the same sort of thing was true with David Copperfield's hands. This was his superpower. He was born to be a magician.

I suddenly became deeply insecure about the size of my hands.

DAN PERES

We took our seats and I placed the tape recorder on the concrete floor between us. Aside from the awkward long handshake,
I managed to keep my cool.

My entire approach to dealing with celebrities had come from
the pep talk about girls Adam had given me when I was fifteen
years old. "You want to be respectful and show interest," he told
me, "but not too much interest. Don't gush. Keep your cool and
act like you belong there."

It may not have gotten me laid, but this advice had served me
well.

In the end, though, I was able to be myself with Copperfield. I
didn't have to pretend to be cooler than I was or more confident or
less interested. He saw to that the moment the interview started.

"Where are you from?" he asked.

I'd done dozens of celebrity interviews by this point, and not
once had anyone ever had any questions for me.

"Did you always want to be a writer?" he asked.

He seemed genuinely curious. He listened as I answered and
shared his own experiences and anecdotes.

"When did you first fall in love with magic?" he asked.

I had wasted little time in letting him know that not only was
I a fan, but that practicing magic, reading about magic, watching
magic—as I had just done earlier that evening—made me feel like
me. Feeling like me—truly being myself—wasn't a regular occur-
rence when I was a kid, I explained. Magic somehow managed to
remove any external pressures and all insecurities, I told him.

"I was the same way," Copperfield said. "I get it. Magic was my
escape, too. It allowed me to be a dreamer. It's important to dream."

This conversation was like a dream. I felt accepted by him.
Patrick, meanwhile, was going to kill me. I had promised to steer
clear of magic, and I spent over an hour talking about it. Screw

it, I figured. This was a once-in-a-lifetime opportunity. I made sure to ask about Schiffer and their engagement toward the end of our interview, and Copperfield gave me more than enough for the story that I needed to write. A story that wouldn't include any of our real conversation, but none of that mattered. The conversation had happened. It was magical.

As we got up to say goodbye, I thanked him for his time and asked if he would mind signing a copy of his new book for me.

"Yes, of course," he said. "I'd be happy to."

I reached into my backpack and pulled out a copy of the book and a pen.

"To Dan Peres," he wrote. "There's no limit to what you can do if you just believe. David Copperfield."

We shook hands—I was sure to let go this time before things got weird—and then he was gone.

The Sheraton was attached to the Hartford Civic Center and it took me only a few minutes to get back to the relative humidity of the fifth floor. I was still buzzing when I walked into my room. The last few bites of my dinner—a cheeseburger and fries—were still on a tray on the room's desk when I walked in. I took a fry, cold and limp, dunked it in ketchup, and popped it in my mouth. It was after 11:30 P.M., but I was far too wired to go to sleep. I sat down on the edge of the bed and pulled the Walkman out of my black JanSport backpack and hit the rewind button—I wanted to listen to our conversation. Relive it.

When I pushed play, though, all I heard was a deep and steady vibration, like the constant hum of an engine. My heart sank. I fast-forwarded the tape a bit and pressed play again. Vibration. I flipped the tape over and tried to listen to the other side. Vibration. My heart was racing. All color drained from my face. I checked the volume. Vibration.

My legs felt weak.

This can't be happening.

I paced around the length of the room. For the second time that night, tears filled my eyes.

And then it hit me. We must have done the interview in a room directly above the industrial machinery that powers the Hartford Civic Center. The tape recorder was on the floor in between me and Copperfield and the rumble that must have been coming from beneath drowned out our voices.

I froze. Then I freaked out.

"No way!" I screamed.

I ripped the bedspread from the bed, sending it and the pillows underneath flying across the room. I swatted the stack of plastic cups into the large windows overlooking the Civic Center and kicked the red upholstered armchair over on its back. My hands shaking, I stopped to try the Walkman again. Vibration. I pounded my fist on the desk and then on the edge of my dinner plate, sending its contents—pickles, fries, a small container of ketchup, and more—into the air and raining down on the bed.

I suddenly regretted not bringing any pills with me to Hartford. I needed to disconnect. To zone out. I even checked my backpack for some, knowing, of course, that they weren't there.

I ultimately took the tape to a sound mixing engineer I found in Manhattan and he was able to separate the vibrations from the voices, allowing me to hear—albeit faintly—my interview with Copperfield.

But that night at the Sheraton, my hotel room in shambles, I listened to both sides of the tape—ninety minutes of low, deep rumbling. It was oddly soothing, in the end. Like a giant purring cat.

I eventually fell asleep next to a small pile of coleslaw.

THE KAVORKA

BARBARA WALTERS IS THE BEST wingman I've ever had.

I met her only once, in Paris in the spring of 1998, but there's no question that she's responsible for my dating one of the most beautiful women in France.

It was one of those perfect late May evenings, the type that makes anyone who's ever lived in Paris forget about the nine months of the year when the skies match the ubiquitous gray sandstone of the city's architecture. The sort of night captured on postcards—dark blue sky with the Seine twinkling in the light of a full moon and the Eiffel Tower glittering in the background. Hollywood's version of Paris.

And there I was, at a party in the kind of apartment off the Avenue Foch that you see only in design magazines, standing in the host's all-white kitchen trying not to get caught staring at Gabrielle, the quintessential Parisian beauty right out of central casting. She was elegant yet pouty. Casual but chic. Both lean and full-figured. She was a cross between Jessica Rabbit and Catherine Deneuve. I was smart enough to know that women like that were best admired from the other side of the room by guys like me. She was, as Adam and Tanner would have readily pointed out, way out of my league.

This wasn't the first time I'd seen Gabrielle. At twenty-four, she was one of the young darlings of Parisian society. Her parents were well-known art collectors and ran a small but important gallery not far from the Bristol Hotel on the tony rue du Faubourg Saint-Honoré. Her unfailingly elegant mother was one of the grande dames of the posh 16th arrondissement and the last of the great chain smokers. Her father always wore a tie, even on weekends, and was dear friends with Fernando Botero, whose bloated bronze sculptures could be found throughout the family's sprawling apartment a short walk from the Place de l'Étoile.

Gabrielle was out nearly every night, one of the "It girls" photographed and featured in the pages of *Paris Match* and France's many glossy fashion magazines. I knew her face well from my tenure as the Eye page editor. We had run her photo in *WWD* and *W* many times. I stood quietly in the kitchen trying to remember something I'd read about her once. She'd had an affair with either a high-ranking French politician or an older American actor she'd met while at the Cannes Film Festival. I couldn't remember which. Either way, I was camped out in the kitchen because I was feeling exceptionally underdressed and most guests had congregated in the apartment's more spacious entertaining rooms.

When I was given the job as the Paris bureau chief for *W* magazine, Patrick McCarthy told me to accept every invitation for the first six months so I could meet as many of the players as possible. And they came pouring in—some by mail, others by fax. That evening's invite came rather casually with a phone call from Sabine, who was the head of couture client relations at a major French fashion house. These jobs were often held by independently wealthy society figures with impressive Rolodexes.

Sabine knew everyone. And if she didn't know someone, then Anna did. And if for some inexplicable reason, neither Sabine nor Anna knew someone, then Benedetta definitely did.

"Okay, I know you're Jewish, but this is your holy trinity," Patrick told me over dinner in Paris the night he introduced me to Sabine, Anna, and Benedetta, whom everyone called Benny.

Sabine oozed elegance. She had been widowed several years earlier when her older investment banker husband had had a stroke on a friend's yacht during the Monaco Grand Prix.

Anna reminded me of Susan Sarandon. She was folksy and carefree and purred, "Ciao, darling," when she kissed you hello in a way that made you think you were the only one she'd ever said that to. She was a countess and divided her time between Paris and Florence, where she managed her family's foundation and was instrumental in convincing billionaires to pay for the restoration of poorly maintained European landmarks.

Benny, meanwhile, had spent fifteen years at Christie's, but just weeks before I moved to Paris, left for Sotheby's in a defection so shocking that it was still being discussed by the Concorde Class well after I arrived. She had a deep, throaty laugh that could be heard across a room and, as I would come to learn, always wore gray.

In their mid-forties, all three were strikingly beautiful and seemed incredibly loyal to Patrick, who must have asked them to look out for me, because I heard from at least one of them every day my first few months in Paris.

"I'm having a little housewarming party," Sabine told me when she called earlier in the week. "It'll be a fun group. Please come."

I was expecting an informal get-together, the kind where people drop in with a bottle of wine in hand, take a look around the new place, eat some cheese, and then take off. I figured jeans and my favorite broken-in navy blue Chuck Taylors would be fine.

A position in the Paris office of Fairchild Publications was considered a plum assignment. John Fairchild himself had run the bureau there in the 1950s, and Patrick was there in the early eighties. A few months before offering me the job, Patrick asked if I would be interested in flying over for the couture shows and to interview Valentino for W.

"I'm not sure I'm the best person to be sitting down with Valentino to discuss design inspiration and fabric choice," I told him.

"Who wants to read a story about that?" asked Patrick. "Not me. Valentino will love you precisely because you're not going to talk to him about fashion."

I had brought a suit with me on that trip, which I wore to a handful of fashion shows, but when I showed up to meet Valentino in his Paris show space on the Place Vendome, I had on a pair of well-worn chinos, a button-down and sweater, and my Chucks. A canvas messenger bag holding a tape recorder and some notes was slung across my chest. As I walked up to the venue, workers were busy unloading lighting trusses and audio equipment from a few small trucks parked diagonally on the sidewalk near the entrance.

"I'm here to see Valentino," I told an official-looking woman with short bangs who was standing by the front door holding a clipboard.

She looked me up and down with obvious disdain, as only the French can, and said something in her native tongue, which I didn't understand.

"Valentino," I repeated. "I'm here to see Valentino."

"Are you the lighting guy?" she asked in heavily accented English. She was wearing a gray pencil skirt and a crisp white shirt. "Your things are being brought in now. Please use the other entrance."

"No. I have a *rendezvous* with *Monsieur* Valentino," I explained, pretty much exhausting the extent of my French.

"Comme ça?" she muttered before reluctantly ushering me in.

A few minutes later, I was standing in front of Valentino. He was wearing a grayish-blue double-breasted suit and perfectly polished brown shoes. He was by far the tannest man I'd ever seen, darker even than my grandfather's friend from Miami Beach, Mort Sugarman, whom I had watched slather baby oil all over himself by the pool at the Carriage House on Collins Avenue when I was a little boy.

"Forgive me if I'm underdressed," I said.

"Not at all," Valentino told me. "You are fresh-faced and very chic."

A few minutes later, while I was sitting on a small sofa next to Valentino as a fitting model twirled in front of us, the woman with the clipboard walked past and we made eye contact. I smiled. She leered.

Comme ça, yourself. He thinks I'm chic, I thought to myself as Valentino talked about the collection he was about to present.

I knew I wasn't chic. Anyone—everyone—who knew me knew I wasn't chic. In fact, when I finally moved to Paris in the fall of 1997 to run W magazine's office there, I was decidedly unchic. My predecessors, on the other hand, had all been incredibly poised and refined women and men. And of course they had all spoken French. At twenty-five, in my Levi's, sneakers, and burgundy North Face fleece and with a knowledge of the language limited to what I'd gleaned from watching Pepé Le Pew reruns on Saturday mornings when I was a kid, I came across more like a hostel-dwelling college student with a Eurail Pass and a dog-eared copy of *Let's Go Europe* than a fashion journalist.

My first few weeks in Paris were as lonely as they were exciting. During the week, when I wasn't at the magazine's well-appointed offices on the rue Royale, I was having lunch with designers from some of the biggest fashion houses in the world. Weeknights were spent attending events and store openings and cocktail parties.

Weekends, however, were quiet. I sometimes hung out with a few other Fairchild transplants from New York, but for the most part I was on my own, wandering around like the new kid in school searching for a seat in the cafeteria—unsure where to go or who to talk to. Cigarettes were my friends, and wontons and General Tso's chicken at a small Chinese place on the rue Saint-Honoré around the corner from the Hôtel Regina, where I was living until I rented an apartment, were dinner most Saturday and Sunday nights. By my third week in Paris, the waitstaff at Café Chinois put my order in the moment I walked through the door.

My favorite waiter was Michel, though I suspected that wasn't his given name. Michel was Chinese but spoke near perfect English thanks to a love of American movies and a Filipino girlfriend who didn't speak French or Mandarin. He went nuts every time I made a sugar cube disappear, using a chopstick as a magic wand, and he was absolutely obsessed with Geena Davis's character, Samantha Caine, in *The Long Kiss Goodnight*. Whenever he would come by to bring me a beer or refill my water glass, he'd ask if I'd seen any pretty girls lately.

"No one as pretty as Samantha Caine," he'd say before I could even answer.

That was debatable. Paris was teeming with beautiful women. Even the women I didn't find attractive seemed to ooze sex appeal just by virtue of their Frenchness. They smoked and drove mopeds and sat outside under heat lamps on chilly evenings sipping wine and speaking . . . French, which, despite its obviousness, I found incredibly sexy. Sometimes, on the way back to my hotel after dinner, I would stop at a café and have a quick drink. I kept waiting

for some sophisticated older woman to hit on me the way Linda
Fiorentino did with Anthony Edwards at a Parisian café in *Gotcha!*,
which I'd seen at least a dozen times when I was a teenager.

In the end, thankfully, I didn't need to wait long. In fact, by the
time I showed up at Sabine's housewarming party the following
spring, my social life had picked up considerably. I had settled into
a small one-bedroom apartment on the rue de Bourgogne in the
7th arrondissement, where several women had already spent the
night. I had, as always, just gotten off to a late start.

Remarkably, it turned out that my arrival in Paris was met with
unexpected enthusiasm by a number of young European women,
particularly junior to midlevel fashion publicists. By my second
month there, many of them had invited me out for drinks and
to non–work-related dinner parties. One Italian woman, Claudia,
who worked in the communications department at Yves Saint
Laurent, even took me on a tour through the streets of Saint-
Germain on the back of her Vespa. I held on for dear life trying
not to shriek like a little girl as she zipped in and out of traffic
pointing out the sights.

I was something of a novelty. I was a young—and despite my
mother's ongoing suspicions—straight man working in an industry
largely devoid of young straight men. I spoke no French, even
though a tutor came to the office twice a week. I can't quite put
my finger on it, but I think I had this almost pathetic lost-puppy
quality that somehow made me desirable. Was this my default
setting? Had I been trying so hard and for so long that I'd never
considered simply not trying at all? Could it have been that simple? This was unfamiliar territory for me in every possible way
and I was mystified by my newfound success with women. So was
Adam, whom I called after each date.

"What is going on over there?" he asked after I told him about my night with Amélie, who had a tousled pixie cut and a small tattoo of a rosary on her hip.

"Holy shit! What are you doing differently?" he demanded to know when I told him about Francesca, an Italian aristocrat living in Paris who took me as a date to a friend's wedding after knowing me for only a week, and once we were there, insisted we sneak into the hotel's indoor pool for my first ever skinny-dip.

"Are you dressing like a Euro dude? Please tell me you're not dressing like a Euro dude," he said when I told him that Sophie unexpectedly pushed me into a darkened banquette at the back of the Hôtel Costes bar, kissed me, and bit my bottom lip so hard I was sure she broke the skin.

But I wasn't doing anything differently, and I certainly wasn't dressing like a Euro dude—no pointy shoes, no painted-on jeans, no slicked back hair. I wore what I always wore: jeans, shirt, Chucks, sometimes even a baseball hat. I had been told more than once that I was *très Américain*, which I knew wasn't necessarily a compliment, but I was *très* comfortable that way and no one seemed to mind.

Most of the time, that is.

That crowd at Sabine's had swelled to about forty people by nine P.M. It was a mix of well-heeled couture clients and their courtly husbands, assorted socialites, and a small handful of Sabine's coworkers. The couture ladies were my favorite. Despite their taut faces and unusually perky breasts, they were what polite society referred to as "women of a certain age." And while spending tens of thousands of dollars on a single dress was serious business, these ladies knew how to have fun. They threw fabulous parties and hung out with rock stars and they welcomed me into their rarefied fold—sneakers and all.

Their husbands, on the other hand, seemed considerably less appreciative of my laid-back sartorial choices. They were captains of industry and the scions of some of Europe's most prominent families. They were, many of them, born with gold-plated poles up their asses and wore arrogance as a facial expression like they were perpetually sucking on lemon wedges. So that evening, after getting more than a few disapproving glances from them, which I assumed were related to my casualness, I retreated to the relative quiet of Sabine's kitchen, where I snacked on puff pastry hors d'oeuvres and did my best to surreptitiously ogle Gabrielle.

I was about to head home when Barbara Walters walked in and started talking about a story in W magazine that she'd read on her flight over from New York. There were ten or so people in the room. Thankfully, everyone was speaking English.

"This article about Marion Lambert was riveting," said Walters. "What a tragedy."

Marion Lambert was a Swiss socialite and the wife of Philippe Lambert, a member of one of Europe's oldest banking families and a cousin of the Rothschilds. Marion's only daughter, Philippine, had committed suicide a few months earlier at the age of twenty, leaving a note accusing an old family friend, a man in his forties with an equally impressive pedigree, of sexually abusing her from the time she was thirteen. He denied the charges. Still mourning, Marion was determined to bring her daughter's alleged rapist to justice, and it sent ripples through the upper echelons of Geneva society. There were many people who felt that Marion was unfairly going after an innocent family man, smearing his name as she blindly crusaded for justice. She had committed the greatest of societal sins— she had aired dirty laundry, and in the process, became a pariah.

"It's tragic, of course, but she doesn't have any proof," one of the couture ladies said to Walters. "She is ruining this man's life."

"Her life has been destroyed," I said from the other side of the room. "And she truly believes that this man abused her daughter."

"Come now," the couture lady said. "How could you possibly know what she truly believes?"

"Because I spent time with her at her house in Geneva," I replied. "I wrote that story."

The room fell silent and all eyes were suddenly on me. Gabrielle's included.

The Marion Lambert article in *W* was one of the first big pieces I did after arriving in Paris. Patrick called me from New York one afternoon and gave me her phone number and backstory and told me to call her. He had never met Marion, but they had a mutual friend who had gotten in touch with him asking for Dominick Dunne's contact information. Marion Lambert was finally ready to break her silence, he was told, and wanted to give an exclusive to Dunne, who had been writing about crime for years at *Vanity Fair*. Patrick did what any good editor would have done. He grabbed the story.

"Dominick Dunne?" he said to his friend. "How about Dan Peres?"

And now one of the most important figures in journalism was talking to me about my story.

"Let's hear from this young man," Walters said. "He's the one who was with her. The one who did the reporting."

While I had Barbara Walters seemingly hanging on my every word and I felt the need to advocate for Marion, whom I had become close with since our interview, all that really mattered in that moment was the fact that Gabrielle was paying attention to me.

I did my best to stay focused on the conversation, which went on for another ten minutes or so, before we were interrupted by a waiter asking that we move to the living room, where one of the sour-faced husbands was about to toast our hostess. It wasn't long after that when I went over to thank Sabine for including me and ask if she wouldn't mind calling me a taxi.

"I can drive you home," I heard someone behind me say. "I'm leaving now also."

It was Gabrielle.

Stay calm. Keep your cool. Close your mouth.

"Are you sure you don't mind?" I asked.

"As long as you don't judge me if my car is messy," she said with a huge smile.

She could have had a corpse in the back seat and I wouldn't have cared. But as luck would have it, I'm not even sure there was a back seat. It was the tiniest car I'd ever seen—a vintage silver Fiat 500, easily as old as I was. As we climbed in, she cleared the passenger seat of a pack of Marlboro Lights, a hairbrush, and one of those cloth drawstring dust bags that come in the box when you buy a nice pair of shoes.

"Sorry, but I can't drive in these heels," she said, as she gently pulled her navy blue silk dress above her knees and effortlessly slipped off her Manolos before pulling a pair of white Chuck Taylors out of the drawstring bag. "We have the same shoes."

Stay calm. Keep your cool. Close your mouth.

We each lit a cigarette as she made her way around the Arc de Triomphe and down the Champs-Élysées toward the Place de la Concorde. When I had envisioned my time in Paris before moving there, this is what I had in mind. Beautiful woman. Cool car. Full moon. If my sixteen-year-old self could have seen me, he wouldn't have believed it. My twenty-five-year-old self was barely accepting it as reality.

"Do you speak French?" she asked.

"Working on it," I replied, "but it's not easy."

"I will teach you," she said. "You can be my student."

Say something smart. Don't fuck this up.

"Okay," I said. That's all I could come up with in the moment. My sixteen-year-old self would have slapped me across the face.

"Have you been to Kinugawa?" she asked, pulling up in front of my apartment. "It's the best sushi in Paris."

I had actually had lunch a few weeks earlier with Karl Lagerfeld at his house in the 7th, and one of the chefs from Kinugawa had come to prepare the meal for us.

"Don't know it," I said.

"Great. Let's have dinner there this weekend," she said. "I'll book the table."

Gabrielle leaned over to me in the passenger seat and gave me a soft kiss on the lips before saying something in French.

"What does that mean?" I asked.

"You'll find out," she said.

At first Adam was convinced I was lying.

"Really? The hottest woman you've ever seen?" he said. "Come on. I know you're on a roll over there, but it's me you're talking to."

"Truth," I said.

"Okay," said Adam. "I've been thinking about this and there's really only one possible explanation for what's been happening to you. You, my friend, have the Kavorka."

The Kavorka was Latvian for "the lure of the animal." Kramer had the Kavorka in the episode of *Seinfeld* where George converts to Latvian Orthodox for the love of a woman. Kramer shows up at the church one day to pick up George, who is there preparing for the conversion, and one of the Latvian Orthodox nuns falls instantly in love with him and wants to leave the faith so she can be with him. The Latvian Orthodox high priest learns of this and tells Kramer that he has the Kavorka.

"Women are drawn to you," the priest explains. "They would give anything to be possessed by you."

Adam and I used to joke about how amazing it would be to have the Kavorka.

And now, at least according to my best friend, I had it.

Maybe he was right.

Gabrielle and I quietly dated for several months, keeping things discreet because she said she didn't want Paris society gossiping about her more than they already were. I didn't mind. I was fine with Gabrielle coming over after a late dinner or meeting her for a drink in dimly lit hotel bars for what she coquettishly referred to as "one last sip before bed."

"This has been a powerful love affair," she said on our last night together. The French even had a way of making breaking up seem sexy.

My two and a half years in France turned out to be one of the most amazing—and truly anomalous—times in my life. There were flings and girlfriends and even the occasional broken heart, but my time in Paris gave me, however briefly, a tenuous sense of confidence—belonging, even—that I had been desperately craving since I was a young boy practicing sleight of hand in my basement in Pikesville. It was as if being desired by women had managed to make me whole—that the Kavorka was somehow the solution to what had eluded me my entire life.

REUNION

WHEN IT COMES TO AIR conditioning and painkillers, the French suck.

They do many things exceptionally well. Better than anyone else, they'll tell you. Like cheese and wine and fashion. They're also rather proud of their philosophers. There are men living in Paris who are philosophers. Not philosophy professors or students or buffs, but actual philosophers. I've met them. And of course the French will insist that their bread is unrivaled—to say nothing of their butter.

They can be forgiven for the air conditioning, which they really seem to be trying to get right—even if everyone isn't fully on board. I know French people who would complain that it was too cold when the AC was on its lightest setting—no joke, like, 80 degrees—and would wrap scarves around their necks and exhale through clenched fists as if they were deckhands on a polar icebreaker.

But when it comes to painkillers, the French truly disappoint.

I discovered this not long before my two and a half years in Paris came to an end.

"You should go to Pitié-Salpêtrière Hospital," Claudio was saying. "It's the best in Paris. It's where they took Princess Diana."

"Yeah, but didn't she die?" I asked.

"Ayy. What's that have to do with anything?" he said.

"I'm just saying, you're trying to convince someone that a hospital is the best in Paris and you make your case by using one of the most famous deaths in the world as an example of their good work," I said. "Not the strongest marketing strategy, no?"

"It's not like they killed her," he said. "Go wherever you want. What do I care?"

We were stoned.

It was a Sunday afternoon and we were sitting outside at Les Deux Magots on the Place Saint-Germain-des-Prés having lunch and watching tourists, all of whom seemed to be carrying money and passports in clear plastic pouches hanging around their necks like oversize tacky necklaces, a fact that made Claudio—with his crisp white shirt, sharply creased slacks, and polished Gucci horsebit loafers—cringe.

He asked if I wanted to smoke a joint first, so I met him at the small, well-appointed Left Bank apartment he shared with his long-time boyfriend, Jean-Yves, who worked as a studio manager for an interior designer favored by Parisian socialites. I watched as Claudio carefully warmed an acorn-sized piece of hash with a lighter before mixing it with tobacco and rolling a thin, perfect joint, complete with a filter he fashioned from a piece torn off of his Marlboro Lights flip-top box.

He was Italian but had been living in Paris for twelve years, where he worked for a global fashion house running communications in France. I met him shortly after I moved to Paris and we would get together once a month to catch up and gossip. We almost always smoked a joint and went to Les Deux Magots, where the famously grumpy, tuxedoed waiters wove through the maze of small round tables and wicker-backed chairs with a noticeable air of disdain for everyone. I could relate.

I'd been telling Claudio over lunch that my back was bothering me and that I was thinking about seeing a doctor. This was only half true. My back was fine, but I'd been fantasizing about Vicodin for the past few weeks and was hoping my friend might be able to recommend a doctor who could help me out.

It had been months since I'd taken my last Vicodin. In fact, since arriving in Paris, I'd used them only periodically, feeding off prescriptions I managed to get from my back surgeon or my longtime physician when I flew to New York a few times a year. Occasional tastes of the buzz I'd fallen in love with before moving, but hardly enough for daily use, which I wasn't craving.

I discovered new kinds of highs while I was in Paris, and I suppose the need to cloak myself in an opiate haze had been replaced by the excitement of the Kavorka and access to—and the acceptance of—people like Karl Lagerfeld and Christian Lacroix and Emanuel Ungaro. For the first time, maybe, I felt wanted. The thrill of my Parisian life had become my drug of choice. That high was enough.

But as with all drugs, the effects eventually fade and you're left foolishly chasing a high that's no longer attainable. That's pretty much where I was the afternoon I sat down at Les Deux Magots with Claudio. It's surprising, frankly, that I went out at all. I think the promise of getting stoned with him was the motivating factor. I had been spending more and more time alone in my apartment on the Boulevard Saint-Germain. The loneliness was only amplified by the fact that I couldn't watch television—the perfect lonely man tonic. Not surprisingly, all programming was in French—episodes of *ER*, *Friends*, even old *M.A.S.H.* reruns—

and despite living in the French capital for several years, I never managed to learn the language. It turned out that Ross's whining to Joey and Chandler about his love for Rachel was just as annoying in French. I'd love to say I tried to master the language, but I never really did. I was a seeker of instant gratification, and the thought of intensive classes at Berlitz wasn't appealing.

By the time I asked Claudio if he could recommend a doctor, I was staying up most nights till dawn, smoking and flipping through the dozens of instructional magic books that lined the white bookshelves I put together in my apartment. They were lopsided. The assembly instructions were in French. I had recently started taking Prozac, which was sent to me after a few phone sessions by a shrink in Baltimore, but all it seemed to do was make me dizzy.

Maybe a little Vicodin in my life could lift me out of my funk?

Despite Claudio's ringing endorsement, I chose not to go to the Princess Diana hospital and instead went to the American Hospital just at the edge of Paris the week after our croque monsieur lunch at Le Deux Magots.

The emergency room smelled of burnt coffee and was empty when I arrived just after eleven A.M. I limped up to the front counter wincing with pain that wasn't there. My "I'm in agony and can barely stand" routine would become Oscar-worthy in the coming years, but was still largely untested at this stage—more improv than rote. I dragged my left leg and grunted with each step as I followed the nurse to an examining room. It's possible I was overselling it a bit, because when we were about ten feet away from the room she stopped, sighed deeply, and gave me what I could have sworn was an eye roll. Or maybe she was just being French. Either way, I dialed the grunting down a notch.

Its inconvenient location notwithstanding, the American Hospital had one tremendous upside—everyone spoke English. My doctor, a short, stocky man in his mid-thirties with several days growth of beard on his face and calm green eyes, spoke perfect English through a strong French accent. He had five pens poking out of his shirt pocket and wore a black Casio calculator watch on his left wrist. He was friendlier than I expected.

"*Alors*, let's have a look," he said, lifting my shirt and gently running his finger over the faded surgery scar on my lower back. This scar would serve as the perfect prop on future doctor visits—verifiable proof that I wasn't entirely full of shit.

I explained how I'd moved to Paris a few months after having had two back surgeries and that my back had been fine for more than two years, but had started hurting recently after I slipped getting out of the bath. Surely this would be believable, as grown men actually took baths in France.

"The pain is almost unbearable," I explained. "When I was in the United States, I took something called Vicodin, and that seemed to help."

"Ah, yes, *bien sur*, Vicodin," he said, nodding.

"I'm not looking to treat my back while I'm here in Paris," I said. "I was just hoping to get enough pain relief until I fly back to New York in a couple of weeks." I had no plans to travel home, but wanted to avoid what I figured might be coming—an MRI, physical therapy, or anything other than pills.

He gave me as thorough an exam as he could, but I didn't make it easy. Every time he asked me to do something—sit, stand, walk across the room, lay flat and lift my legs to a 90-degree angle—I would stop midway and clutch my back.

"I know I can do it," I said. "I just need a second to rest."

"No. No. Please don't hurt yourself," the doctor said. "Let's see what we can do for the pain."

Wow. That was easy.

"Like I said, Vicodin was very helpful when I took it in New York," I offered—again.

"We don't have Vicodin here," he replied.

"Of course," I said, standing up and slowly tucking in my shirt. "I'm not sure what you call it here, but maybe something like that."

"There is nothing like that in France," he said.

"Maybe you're not understanding," I suggested. "Vicodin is a painkiller."

"Yes, I know what Vicodin is," he said. "I was premed at Chapel Hill."

Oh. Okay.

"We don't have drugs like that here in France," he explained. "The closest thing we have is Efferalgan Codeine, which is essentially the same thing as Tylenol with Codeine, which is not as powerful as Vicodin. That's the strongest analgesic pain reliever you can get outside of a hospital. I can give you a prescription for it."

There are pharmacies on every corner in this country and the strongest painkiller they have is Tylenol with Codeine? What a tease. I didn't want something weaker than I had already taken in the past. That wasn't going to get me where I desperately needed to go.

"Do you really think it'll help?" I asked, making a particularly strong show of how hard I was trying to get my shoes back on.

"If you'd like, I can give you a shot of morphine today to see if we can quiet down some of the pain," the doctor said. "You'd have to stay here for four hours, though. Are you driving?"

"No, I took a taxi," I said. "Sure, I'll try that."

I barely felt the injection. The nurse shut the lights and told me she'd be by to check on me shortly. I could hear the whine of a euro-siren approaching the building and the squeak of sneakers coming and going in the hallway.

I waited.

"Was this a mistake?" I wondered.

I had my answer about ten minutes later.

And just like that, I was floating. Levitating over the creaky hospital bed like I was in one of David Copperfield's grand illusions—soaring out over the crowd like a spellbound volunteer from the audience. No fear. I was warm and relaxed and—for the first time in months—comfortable in my own skin.

I was home.

Little did I know, I'd be home for real before the end of the month.

Patrick called and asked me to fly back to New York to discuss the possibility of taking over *Details*. I was offered the position and immediately tasked with rebuilding the magazine.

I was twenty-eight, back in New York with an exciting high-profile job, and about to begin my next powerful love affair—one that nearly killed me.

UNRAVELING, PART II

I LIKED THAT THEY knew me.

I'd been staying at the Morgans Hotel on Madison Avenue for several weeks already, and every time I walked inside, someone was saying my name.

Aspiring actor doormen, with their cleft chins and soap-star good looks, swung the doors open well before I even reached them.

"Welcome back, Mr. Peres."

The fresh-faced men and women working the front desk, lean in fitted gray sweaters, smiled every time I passed through the small, fragrant lobby.

"There's a fax for you, Mr. Peres."

"Cold out there, isn't it, Mr. Peres?"

"We ran a package up to your room, Mr. Peres."

It may have been the first time—other than some self-important high school teacher or one of my mom's drunken friends at my bar mitzvah—that anyone had ever called me Mr. Peres. I liked it. I never once told them to call me Dan.

My room was actually several rooms—a one-bedroom suite on the seventeenth floor that I'd been living in since moving back from Paris to take the *Details* job. There was a big living room with a powder room and a large separate bedroom. An upholstered banquette sat in front of a bank of windows facing west. The room was bright with afternoon light. There was a polished wooden tray on the marble-topped minibar packed with snacks from Dean & DeLuca—savory cheese sticks, hickory-smoked almonds, the world's softest gummy bears—wrapped in small crinkly plastic bags.

The room was decorated in soft neutral colors—light grays and cream. The only real contrast in the hotel suite came from a black-and-white-checked blanket folded neatly across the foot of the bed. I brought one bag with me from Paris—everything else was being shipped—and my clothes were neatly in place in a small wood-lined walk-in closet in the bedroom.

It was the most luxurious suite I'd ever stayed in, and in February of 2000 it became the site of my second hotel-room trashing.

I'd first heard of the Morgans Hotel during my freshman year of college. My girlfriend Rachel's wealthy aunt Becca used to stay there when she visited from Beverly Hills. We picked her up there once on our way to a fondue place uptown. The paparazzi were gathered out front waiting for celebrities. I remember thinking that was the coolest thing I'd ever seen. It was even cooler than seeing Matt Dillon and Sean Young right outside of my freshman dorm on lower Fifth Avenue one night while they were shooting a scene from some forgettable movie. (Dillon asked out one of the girls on my floor while she was outside watching them film, making her something of a celebrity at Rubin Hall.)

I pretended to know who Ian Schrager and Steve Rubell were when Becca explained that the legendary founders of Studio 54 were the ones who'd opened the hotel a few years earlier. I also pretended to know what Studio 54 was. Becca loved the Morgans because it was a small hotel, she said, but it offered all of the luxuries of one of the old-school five-star places that she hated on the Upper East Side. Celebrities loved it, too. It was quiet and indistinctive on a nondescript block on lower Madison Avenue. It was the first boutique hotel. And now it was my new address while I settled back into New York and into my new role as editor in chief of *Details*.

I didn't expect to be staying there long. In fact, I didn't expect to be given the *Details* job in the first place. What did I know about running a magazine?

While the W Paris job came with a great title, European Editor, I was essentially just a glorified features writer and schmoozer of designers and socialites. I was hardly responsible, and if I made it into the office before eleven A.M., it was a shock to those who'd already been there for hours. But I wasn't complaining. I traveled wherever I wanted for stories—London, Geneva, Berlin, Gstaad. I flew on private planes with billionaires, hung out on yachts during the Monaco Grand Prix, and had long flirty lunches with ridiculously rich women I was trying to convince to showcase their opulent Parisian pieds-à-terre in the pages of W. It didn't even matter that most of them were in their seventies. I once got drunk on 200-year-old cognac with an eccentric French baron—in the middle of the day. "You should have some, my young friend," the baron said after I politely passed. "It's from the French Revolution. You understand? Napoleon was alive when this was made." I stumbled home.

It was the ideal job for me—high profile enough to make me feel important, but extremely light on responsibility.

I wasn't ready for any real responsibility. I was, however, desperate to get out of Paris, and the idea of being the editor of *Details* had appealed to me long before I was ever even offered the job. About two years before I moved to Paris, I was having dinner one night at the tony Greenwich Village eatery Il Cantinori when the restaurant's manager brought the chef over to meet the man dining at the next table. "This is the editor in chief of *Details*," he said as he introduced the two men. The chef shook the editor's hand enthusiastically and personally brought out three dishes for him and his raven-haired date to sample. With each visit to the table, the chef described the dish and its Tuscan inspiration and offered a warm "*buon appetito!*"

I wanted that. Not the food as much as the attention, though free carpaccio is always a bonus. I was hungry for validation. I had a long-simmering desire to be both noticed and invisible at the same time. This was my struggle—the bizarre by-product of a crippling insecurity and an inflated ego. Getting the *Details* job fed both.

"GOOD AFTERNOON, MR. PERES," the woman behind the front desk at the Morgans chirped as I walked in. "There's a gentleman waiting for you." She pointed over to the brown leather club chair on the other side of the room where Ivan was sitting. There was a black-and-white-checked blanket draped over the back of the chair. Ivan was reading a copy of the quarterly literary journal the *Paris Review*. That, and the fact that he had a soul patch— a brittle tuft of rust-colored hair dangling from his bottom lip like a weather-beaten Christmas wreath still hanging on a front door in April—made me dislike him immediately.

"I'm so sorry I'm late," I said, hand outstretched as I crossed the small lobby to greet him. "I just moved back to New York and had forgotten that taking a taxi down Fifth Avenue in the middle of the day is a horrible idea."

Ivan was there to see me about a job, just one in a wave of editors, writers, and art directors I'd been meeting since I became editor in chief of *Details* a few weeks earlier. *Details* was founded in the early eighties and was bought by Condé Nast in 1989. In the early to mid-nineties, the magazine had developed a strong cultural voice and a sizable audience. I even applied for a job there after graduating from NYU but was sent the standard rejection letter informing me that there were no positions available at that time but that they would keep my résumé on file. *Details* was cool and insidery and downtown. It was hardly the right fit for me anyway. So I took the job at *DNR* writing about cable-knit sweaters and covering the National Retail Federation—admittedly not the coolest or most stylish group of guys, but there were some pretty innovative takes on the comb-over within their ranks.

Details had had a handful of editors in chief since the mid-nineties, and by the time I was given the job in 2000, its once untouchable cool factor had faded thanks to a colossal shift in the men's magazine market toward babes and bathroom humor that came sweeping in from England with the popularity of magazines like *Maxim* and *FHM*. Beneath their perfectly fitted bespoke suits and shiny oxfords, the Brits were really giant pervs. Edginess and cool had given way to T&A and bosomy midriff-baring cover models. Fighting to compete, most traditional men's magazines, including *Details*, followed suit, and their covers became virtually indistinguishable from the *Playboy*s I used to try to peek at as a kid while pretending to look for comic books when I was at the Rite Aid in the Greenspring Shopping Center with my mom. In the end, though, that type of magazine just didn't fit in with the overall Condé Nast brand ethos of luxury and sophistication. Shortly before I moved back from Paris, the powers that be at Condé Nast decided to shut *Details* down, turn it over to Fairchild, which the company had recently acquired, and relaunch it.

"They tried taking the *Maxim* route, but it didn't work," Patrick explained when we were talking about what to do with *Details*. "It needs to be different. Sophisticated. Smarter than the rest."

I thought there might be some opportunity for me to take a senior role when Patrick called me at my office in Paris and told me he'd like for me to fly to New York to discuss *Details*, but I never expected to be given *the* job. In the end, I think it came down to the fact that Patrick knew and trusted me and recognized that I shared his flair for colorful storytelling. It certainly wasn't my leadership experience. I had never managed more than a small handful of people and had never hired—or fired—anyone. I was underqualified, for sure, but I did have some ideas of what a modern men's magazine should look like.

"There's nothing out there for men who are smart and stylish but aren't interested in having a magazine sitting on their coffee table that has a woman in a wet T-shirt on the cover," I told Patrick. "That feels like such a lowest-common-denominator approach to speaking to men. Let's face it . . . not all guys come to a magazine to read about beer, barbecue, and babes. I know plenty of men who are interested in design and architecture and art and fashion."

I had been living in Paris for the last three years surrounded by men in the fashion business—men who didn't need wives or girlfriends or mothers to tell them what clothes to buy and how they should decorate their homes. They were elegant and confident. They cooked and collected art. They wore cashmere scarves looped coolly around their necks on chilly days instead of wearing coats. And they most definitely wouldn't have been caught dead in a pair of corduroys embroidered with tiny whales.

"*Details* needs to defy stereotypes," I told Patrick. "It can't be too straight or too gay. It needs to walk that fine line in between."

"Let's do it," said Patrick.

When Condé Nast closed *Details* about a month earlier, the entire staff had been let go. I had to hire thirty people as quickly as I could, and I had never conducted a job interview in my life. Now I had a stack of résumés in my suite at the Morgans and had been meeting people, sometimes three or four a day, for several weeks. This had been an ego-fueling process, but it had also been incredibly stressful. Most of the people I met with were older than me, and they were all far more experienced. I did my best to hide my insecurity behind a veil of cooked-up confidence.

I did what I'd always done. I pretended.

It wasn't traffic that made me late for Ivan, who, as it turned out in what would be the final blow for his prospects as a future *Details* editor, pronounced his name *E-von*. I was coming from a doctor's appointment.

I'd been seeing Dr. Irwin Rosenbaum for an annual physical since my days at NYU. He was a heavyset man in his late fifties with a constellation of skin tags on his neck and hands the size of baseball mitts. He was the doctor who discovered I had only one kidney after questioning why lab results indicated that I had a higher than average red blood cell count. Dr. Rosenbaum was a Modern Orthodox Jew with offices on Fifth Avenue and 84th Street and in Great Neck, Long Island, where he lived with his wife and three sons. Pictures of his kids dressed in matching navy polo shirts, khakis, and blue yarmulkes—one with the Yankees logo stitched in white on the front—hung on one of the waiting-room walls. The photos had to have been more than ten years old, as they showed young boys who I now knew to be college age or older. I'd called to schedule a physical the day before, but was given a next-day appointment due to a cancellation.

From the time I was a little boy, I always loved going to the doctor. I loved the smell of the doctor's office—a potpourri of disinfectant, latex, and lollipops, with just a hint of urine. The vinyl furniture that exhaled a poof of air and dust whenever I sat. The well-worn copies of *Highlights* magazine with the address labels torn off that my mother forbade me to touch. "Daniel Peres, put that down this instant," she'd scold. "Do you know how many snotty noses have dripped on that?"

I loved waiting in the examining room, too. The way the nurse would slip the manila folder with my name written across the front into a plastic file holder mounted to the outside of the door as she showed me inside. I made up magic tricks using the cotton balls and tongue depressors that sat in large glass jars on the counter next to a box of rubber gloves and—the most thrilling of all examining-room items—the knee hammer. Up on the table I'd go, a thin layer of white paper crinkling beneath me, fruitlessly hammering away at my own knees.

I felt at home at the doctor's office. Comfortable. Happy, even.

My pediatrician, Dr. Layton, made me feel like a celebrity every time I was there, pointing out, not just to me but to his entire office staff, that I was his first newborn patient. "He talks about you like he gave birth to you," my mother said once. Dr. Layton was a kind and gentle man with a soft voice and warm hands, but the most interesting thing about him—to a young boy like me, anyway—was the fact that his first name was Dick. This was a source of endless amusement for me and my brother, Jeff. "Are we going to see Dick today?" we'd ask our mother from the back seat of the car, trying to contain our laughter. "He's such a nice man," we'd say. "Does everyone like Dick?"

Going to the doctor also meant attention. It put me front and center. I used to secretly wish that the doctor would discover I had asthma or some other quasi-serious but non–life-threatening ailment that might get me some sympathy . . . or at least get me out of gym. Plus, I always thought inhalers were super cool. I loved a prop.

Between the ages of ten and fourteen, I spent summers at sleepaway camp in Maine, where I no doubt spent more time with the nurse, Katrina, in the infirmary than I did with my bunkmates in the lake. The infirmary was one of the few buildings—really just a wood cabin only slightly larger than the bunks that lined the dirt path next to the soccer field—that had air conditioning. Everyone called Katrina "Olive Oyl," though not to her face, because she was unusually tall and rail-thin. She had shoulder-length black hair, which she wore in a ponytail, and she didn't dress like the nurses in Dick's office. She wore OP shorts, baggy T-shirts, and a red fanny pack where she kept Band-Aids, antiseptic wipes, Bacitracin, and a pair of medical scissors that were bent in the middle and rounded at the edges. Though I was never able to confirm it, she was widely rumored to have had hairy armpits. Poison ivy, headaches, a twisted ankle, even the occasional splinter—I'd find any reason I could to go see Katrina. Being in the infirmary is one of the most enduring memories I have of summer camp.

I made quite an entrance when I walked into Dr. Rosenbaum's office the day I was late for my meeting with *E-von*. Patrick had arranged for me to get a discount at Giorgio Armani, where I'd gone a few days earlier to buy two new suits and a pair of black lace-up shoes. After all of my talk about elegance and sophistication, I figured I should walk the walk. What I didn't realize was that the soles of my new Armani shoes were made of polished leather, which made walking any walk a challenge. I slid across Dr. Rosenbaum's waiting room like I was trying to beat a tag at third base.

"Whoa," said Dr. Rosenbaum, who was standing next to the receptionist, scribbling notes in a file. "The prodigal son returns," he said. "All that time in France and you come home doing pratfalls better then Jerry Lewis. He's like a god over there, right?"

I made two split-second decisions as I was getting up off of the waiting-room floor. The first was to go back to wearing my uniform of jeans and sneakers. I may have been pretending to be an editor in chief, but dressing the part had just taken a dangerous and embarrassing turn. My second decision was to pretend that I'd really hurt my back, which despite the Lewis-esque slip was fine. I don't really even remember thinking about it. I just did it—as if it were an involuntary action, like blinking. I stood slowly, clutched my back, and let out a soft but audible groan.

"This is just what I need," I said, limping up to the counter the same way I had down the marble hallway at the American Hospital in Paris weeks earlier. "I definitely just did something to my back."

"Do you want to lie down in one of the exam rooms?" Dr. Rosenbaum asked. "I have one patient ahead of you. Shouldn't be too long."

"I probably should. My back is hurting," I said, repeating the claim for maximum impact.

Despite stopping at three pharmacies the day before I left Paris, including one at Delta terminal in Charles de Gaulle, to stock up on the effervescent painkiller that I'd been given when I left the American Hospital, Efferalgan Codeine, I was down to my last package. It turned out that French pharmacies gave the doctor's prescription back to you after filling it. I think they were supposed to stamp it with the date, but they never did—something I didn't take issue with. This medicine was fairly common in France and was barely regulated—it had actually been sold over the counter up until a year or so earlier, making France an addict's dream destination. I would later learn that you could also get it without a prescription in London, which would come in handy in the years to come.

I hadn't been sleeping well since my return to New York. At first I chalked it up to jet lag, but I was beginning to feel the anxieties of the new job and the responsibilities that came with the business card. Who knew that working full days would be so stressful?

A day or two after I landed in New York, I ran into a colleague, Merle Ginsberg, who had been dividing her time between working for W and Los Angeles magazine, which had been recently acquired by Fairchild. The new editor in chief of Los Angeles magazine, Spencer Beck, was also a former W editor whom I'd known for years.

"Let me ask you a question," I said while catching up with Merle in the massive newsroom at the Fairchild offices. "As an editor in chief, is Spencer there every day? Is he there all day?"

"What are you talking about?" she asked. "He's running the magazine. He's there around the clock."

I was crestfallen.

The Efferalgan Codeine was helping me unwind at night. I'd drop two into the small bottle of Evian water the housekeeper at the Morgans would leave on the nightstand and chug it before climbing into bed. It helped. After being back in New York for about ten days, a week or so before my physical with Dr. Rosenbaum, I decided to take a couple in the middle of the day. It was a Saturday, with no meetings scheduled, so I figured the Efferalgan Codeine might help me nap. I didn't. Instead, I felt a slight buzz and sat on the sofa in the living room of my suite smoking cigarettes and watching back-to-back episodes of Diff'rent Strokes. It was the most relaxed I'd been since moving back.

"I read about your new job in the Post," Dr. Rosenbaum said

as he settled on a stool across from me in the examining room. "You're a star."

"I wouldn't go that far," I said, "but it's definitely exciting."

After my checkup, I asked the doctor if he could give me something for my back. Dr. Rosenbaum had written me a prescription for a hundred Extra Strength Vicodin just before I moved to Paris—an "emergency supply" in case anything happened. I reminded him of this and asked for the same, making a point to groan in pain while lacing up my slippery new shoes.

"How about sixty?" he asked, pulling a prescription pad from the saggy side pocket of his white lab coat. I knew this wasn't a negotiation, but said, "Make it eighty and we've got a deal."

I took the prescription for sixty Extra Strength Vicodin and made my way back to the Morgans, where E-von and his soul patch were patiently waiting. I'd been given a desk at the Fairchild headquarters on 34th Street, but I did most of the interviews either in my suite at the Morgans or at the bar in Asia de Cuba, the hotel's trendy restaurant just off the lobby and downstairs.

E-von and I made our way to Asia de Cuba, where he told me that his favorite writers were Saul Bellow and Thomas Pynchon—two men whose work I had attempted to read on several occasions but had given up on after a few pages. He was hoping to discover the next generation of literary giants and thought *Details* would be the perfect place to showcase their work, he explained.

Oh, boy.

"Well, E-von, I really appreciate you coming by today," I told him after wearily listening to twenty minutes on literary theory. "I apologize again for being late, but unfortunately I have another meeting in a few minutes and need to run."

My next meeting wasn't for another few hours, but I wanted to change out of my suit and the Armani roller skates and get to the

Duane Reade on the corner of 34th and Fifth to have my prescription filled. I was looking forward to how the Vicodin were going to make me feel. I wove my way through the throngs of tourists clogging the sidewalks with the nervous excitement of a six-year-old kid pushing through a crowded mall to sit on Santa's lap for the first time.

The opaque orange prescription bottle was larger than I expected. I could feel it through the small white bag that the pharmacist had stapled shut. Maybe he accidently gave me more pills, I thought hopefully. Once in the privacy of my hotel suite, I tore the bag open and placed the bottle on the coffee table next to a pile of résumés and some back issues of *Details*. *Take 1–2 tablets by mouth every 4–6 hours as needed for pain. Qty: 60. No refills.* I gazed at the label for a moment before removing the cap and spilling three or four chalky white oval pills into the palm of my hand. Each had *Watson 3203* imprinted in it. I stared at them like a fortune-teller studying a handful of crystals.

Should I?

My final meeting of the day wasn't with a job candidate, but instead with a publicist, Kelsey Brown, who had asked me out for a drink to hear my plans for the magazine and tell me about some of her celebrity clients.

Should I? I thought as I contemplated the pills. This is a casual meeting, right? A publicist looking to suck up to me for coverage in a magazine that doesn't even exist yet. What's the big deal?

I popped three in my mouth and swallowed them with a large gulp of Diet Coke. I grabbed a bag of Dean & DeLuca cheese sticks from the minibar and headed off to meet Kelsey for a drink at Keens Steakhouse on 36th Street, which was about a ten-minute walk from the Morgans.

I first met Kelsey when I was working as a reporter for *WWD*'s

Eye page and she was a junior publicist for PMK, the powerhouse celebrity PR firm that had an impressive roster of movie stars, many of whom I was hoping to land for the cover of *Details*. I had recently decided that the magazine would feature only men on its covers as a way to distinguish *Details* from the pack, and Kelsey, who had climbed the ranks at PMK, now represented some of the top leading men in Hollywood.

Keens was a carnivore's delight—an over hundred-year-old Manhattan landmark known as much for its Flintstone-sized steaks and mutton chops as for its collection of tens of thousands of long, skinny wooden pipes that lined the ceiling. Kelsey was sitting in the dark, wood-paneled bar drinking a white wine spritzer and talking on her cell phone when I showed up. She had long, wavy strawberry-blond hair and a round, full baby face punctuated with faded brownish-red freckles. Though she was in her early thirties, it wouldn't have surprised me to learn that the bartender asked for ID before serving her.

"I always knew you were going to be an editor in chief," she said as she hopped off her stool to give me a hug. She was still on the phone. "Just wrapping up a call to the coast," she said.

I always hated the way that people in entertainment referred to Los Angeles as "the coast," as if it was the only place in the country that bordered an ocean.

As we were catching up, I felt the familiar sensation of the Vicodin taking effect—like slowly being lowered into a warm bath. Only more enveloping. More buoyant. Like a bath of warm milk, maybe. I didn't realize how much I had missed this feeling.

I drifted away from the conversation for a moment while Kelsey was rattling off a list of client names she was reading from a small laminated card she had produced from her purse. I was floating. Tingling. I had to force myself back into reality and regain my fo-

AS NEEDED FOR PAIN

cus. I wasn't sure I'd heard what she'd said and asked her to repeat the name she just read.

"David Copperfield," she said.

I was back.

"Really?" I said. "I'm a huge fan. I actually interviewed him once about five years ago."

"That's great," said Kelsey. "I'm sure he'd love to do the cover."

I could only imagine how that conversation with Patrick would go.

"I don't see him as a cover subject, if I'm being honest, but I do think he's amazing," I said.

"I should get you guys together," she said excitedly. "He's back in New York at the beginning of next week."

"Absolutely," I said. "One hundred percent."

"Oh my god, you have to go to his apartment," Kelsey said. "You won't believe the apartment."

Early the following week, I'm standing in an elevator on my way to the penthouse of an exclusive midtown high-rise. My ears pop as the car climbs to the fifty-seventh floor, where the doors open to a spacious lobby. To the left are a set of glass doors leading to a roof deck for the residents of the tony condo. To the right is a large wooden door—the only apartment on the floor. I take a deep breath to calm my nerves and ring the bell.

The door swings open and David Copperfield is standing there in a pair of dark jeans, a black button-down shirt, and black socks. He's not wearing shoes. He looks exactly the same as he did five years earlier when I met him in Hartford, except for his hair. It's still big on top—volume, my mother would say—but it's shorter in the back. Poof . . . the Jewish mullet had magically disappeared.

"Hey, Dan. Good to see you," he said softly. "Come on in."

Kelsey was right. The apartment was like nothing I'd ever seen before—an almost indescribable combination of elegance and luxury and taste mixed with bizarre curios and games and one-of-a-kind collectibles spread out across four levels. P. T. Barnum meets Jean-Michel Frank. A sprawling apartment that would be equally at home in the pages of both *Architectural Digest* and *Mad* magazine. And all with 360-degree views of New York City.

"I doubt you remember," I said as we climbed a sweeping staircase to the two-story living room, which had a life-size artist's mannequin dangling from the thick chain holding the chandelier. "But I interviewed you a few years ago for a story I wrote in *W*."

"Of course I remember," he said. He was being polite. "Do you want to see something cool?" As if being in David Copperfield's apartment wasn't already cool enough.

"Sure," I said.

He told me to sit in what looked to be a wooden chair. A dozen or so wooden figures—antique marionette forms, David explained—were attached to the wall of the fireplace. Several large Klieg lights, no doubt salvaged and restored from the golden age of Hollywood, stood on tripods on either side of two cream-colored sofas. The room was light and airy.

"You don't by any chance have a bad back, do you?" he asked.

"Nope," I said. Despite the performance I put on for Dr. Rosenbaum the previous week, my back had never felt better. There was no point in lying to Copperfield, I figured. It's not like he could write me a prescription.

"Good," he said.

A second later, I was flat on my back, the antique chair broken beneath me. I looked up to see David standing over me, smiling, holding the string he had pulled to collapse the chair. "Cool, right?" It was.

We settled in his rich, mahogany-paneled study on the mezzanine of the apartment. Paintings of dogs dressed as humans—one in a nun's habit—hung above the fireplace.

"Kelsey told me that you just moved back from Paris," he said. "Are you excited about the new job?"

"I am," I said. "But I'm nervous. It's a big job. It's keeping me up at night." I was becoming a seasoned liar, yet here I was telling the truth to David Copperfield. I felt safe—as safe as I had as a young boy performing magic tricks to an imaginary audience next to the pool table in my basement, VHS tapes of his television specials playing in the background.

An antique ventriloquist's dummy was leaning against the wall on the other side of the room, looking right at me. I shifted on the sofa.

"I get it," he said. "People are paying attention now. You're in the spotlight."

"I've always wanted to be in the spotlight, I guess," I told him. "But then again, not really. Does that make sense? Now that I'm there, I'm not so sure it's for me."

"Tell me about it," he said with a laugh.

"Were you ever scared that you wouldn't be able to do what you set out to do?" I asked.

"Fear of failure is normal," he said. "We all deal with fear."

I felt the blood rushing to my head, my face getting flushed. For some reason I wanted to cry, though I wasn't sure why. David Copperfield had always been my escape. My disconnect from reality. Watching those videos of his TV specials in my basement had always made me feel comfortable and at ease. They made me feel like myself. I suppose all of the pretending I'd been doing was somehow taking its toll on me. I had figured David might be able to make me feel better as he had so many times before. I looked over at an antique wooden mask resting on the mantel. I wanted to hide behind it. I exhaled deeply and casually wiped my sweaty palms on my pants.

"Listen, you're going to be great," David added. "You wouldn't have been given the job if the right people didn't think so. But any time you want to talk, you should give me a call."

He leaned over to grab a small piece of paper and a pen from a table next to the sofa and scribbled down two phone numbers— one for him and the other for his assistant.

"I'll be back in New York in a couple of weeks," he told me. "Let's get dinner. I'll get your number from Kelsey."

I'm not sure what I was expecting to happen that afternoon. For a moment earlier in the day, I'd even been considering how to let him down gently if he asked to be on the cover of my magazine. I was well aware that my fondness for David Copperfield and magic wasn't necessarily the right fit for *Details*. But he never asked. He didn't even hint at it. It turns out that the afternoon wasn't about that. My visit to his apartment wasn't about him at all.

I walked back to the hotel, took two Vicodin, and climbed into bed. It was six P.M.

"THERE'S A BUTTON on the floor under the desk that allows you to close the office door," my new assistant, Trish, was saying a few days later. "Just don't ever slam it in my face, please."

I'd spent the morning looking at apartments in the Village with my friend Adam and was now touring *Details*'s temporary offices on Madison Avenue, where we'd been given half of a floor in the old Condé Nast headquarters until space could be made for us in the Fairchild building on 34th Street. There were ten or so window offices, a large conference room in the center of the floor with frosted-glass windows, and a few dozen cubicles. I'd already hired eight people, a few of whom were going to be starting the following Monday. Trish and I were just getting the lay of the land and making a rough seating chart when Scott, the front-desk manager from the Morgans, called.

"Sorry to bother you, Mr. Peres," Scott said. "Unfortunately, we're going to have to move you from the suite you've been in for the last three weeks and into another, slightly smaller suite on the fourteenth floor."

Apparently, there had been a long-standing reservation for my suite beginning that night, he explained, but due to a computer error, no one realized that it was double booked. He apologized for not telling me sooner and asked if I'd mind if housekeeping moved my things to the new room. I'd seen an apartment on 11th Street earlier that day that I liked and figured my days at the Morgans were numbered anyway, so I told Scott I didn't—a decision I'd come to regret a few hours later.

"Welcome back, Mr. Peres," the doorman said as I approached the hotel. "The front desk asked me to remind you to stop by and get a new key."

The new suite was noticeably smaller and didn't have a second bathroom, but there was a gift basket on the coffee table overflowing with bags of the Dean & DeLuca cheese sticks and gummy bears along with a note from Scott thanking me for understanding, which more than made up for it. I grabbed a Diet Coke from the minibar and went to the bathroom to take the Vicodin I'd been craving all day.

The pill bottle wasn't there.

A sudden feeling of panic came over me. I looked in my black nylon Dopp kit that was sitting on the bathroom counter—razor, shaving cream, an empty container of Efferalgan Codeine, nail clippers, and about dozen white plastic collar stays, but no bottle. My heart racing, I went out into the bedroom to check the night-stands. Not there. The walk-in closet was also smaller—more of an alcove—but it wasn't in there, either. I took my clothes off the shelves. Nothing. I pulled my suitcase out, but there was nothing but dirty laundry and the Armani shoes. I looked under the bed and behind the pillows, scoured the living room. Everything else was there—the files of résumés and writing samples. The old copies of *Details* and the current issues of *GQ*, *Esquire*, and *Maxim* I'd been looking at. Even the half-eaten pack of Twizzlers and the Asia de Cuba matchbook I'd left on the coffee table of the old suite were there. No pills.

"This is Mr. Peres," I said calling the front desk. I was having trouble catching my breath. "You guys moved my things to a new room today and I can't find my medication. It was right on the sink in my old room and it's not here."

Two minutes later, Scott and the housekeeping manager, a woman in her mid- to late thirties wearing a light brown pantsuit and holding a leather notebook portfolio, were at my door.

"I need my medication," I said when they walked in. "Who packed my things?"

"Mr. Peres, I'm so sorry," said Scott. "We'll find it."

"Who packed my things?" I asked, raising my voice.

"It would have been someone from housekeeping and one of the bellmen," he said. "I'm sure it's here. Can we help you look?"

"Get the people that moved my things up here right now," I demanded.

"Mr. Peres, please calm down," said Scott.

"Don't tell me to calm down," I said. "I need my medication. This is unacceptable. Get the people who moved my things up here now."

"The housekeeping shift would have changed at five P.M.," he said. "The bellman is probably still here. Let me call him."

The bellman arrived and explained that he only loaded my things on the luggage cart and took them to the new room, but the housekeeper did the actual packing and unpacking.

"I knew it. The housekeeper stole my medication," I announced, throwing my hands up in the air.

Scott and the housekeeping manager just looked at me, their heads slightly cocked. The bellman looked away when I made eye contact with him.

"Find the housekeeper," I said. "I want to talk to her."

"Mr. Peres . . . please," Scott said calmly after a long pause. "Why don't we go check your old room?"

"Let's," I said. "And I don't care if there are people in there. We're going in."

The suite was still empty. There was a bottle of wine and a plate of chocolates waiting on the coffee table with a note to welcome the new guests. The shades were drawn and soft jazz was playing on the radio. The room was dimly lit and smelled of lemon-scented air freshener.

Scott and the housekeeping manager walked briskly through the suite. I followed them as they darted from the living room to the powder room to the bedroom to the bathroom, opening and closing drawers and checking trash cans as they went. My heart was pounding and I was breathing heavily.

"It doesn't seem to be here," said the housekeeping manager.

"Mr. Peres, I'm terribly sorry about this," Scott said. "The hotel has a doctor on call. Perhaps we can call him for you and he can replace the missing medication. The hotel would cover all costs, of course."

"Are you fucking kidding me?" I said, pushing past him and

going back into the bedroom. "We're not done looking in this room. And has anyone even tried to find that housekeeper?"

"Sir, I understand that you're upset," he said, "but it's not here."

"Yeah, well, I'm going to take a closer look," I said. "Maybe the bottle rolled behind the bed or something."

I walked over to the side of the bed, gripped on the frame and pulled. It didn't move.

"Mr. Peres, the bed is mounted to the wall," said Scott, who had followed me.

"Come on!" I said, knocking the pillows to the floor and throwing the black-and-white-checked throw blanket over my right shoulder. "This is fucking ridiculous."

I walked over to the window seat, tossed three tan bolster cushions onto the bed, and pulled the main cushion to the floor.

"Mr. Peres," Scott said firmly. "I realize that you're upset, but we've checked this room."

"Bullshit," I yelled. "Looking into empty trash cans doesn't count."

I stormed into the bathroom, sweeping a stack of neatly folded white bath towels off a metal rack and onto the floor.

"I need my medicine," I said. "You don't seem to understand."

Scott stood silently by the window seat.

"Did anyone bother to check behind the nightstands?" I said, yanking the small table away from the wall and sending a skinny silver lamp and the phone crashing to the floor.

"Sir, I'm going to have to ask you to leave the room," said Scott.

"You guys suck," I said, kicking over the small mesh trash can that had been under the desk but that either Scott or the house-keeping manager had left in the doorway. I walked into the hall.

"I understand this is a tremendous inconvenience, Mr. Peres," said Scott, now trailing behind me. "Can we arrange for you to see the doctor?"

"No," I said. "And don't just stand here looking at me while I wait for the elevator. I want to be alone."

"Of course," he said, turning and walking away.

"Wait a minute," I said, calling after him. "What floor is my new room on again?"

Back in my room on the fourteenth floor and still breathing heavily and sweating, I lit a cigarette and sat on the sofa to check my cell phone for messages. I'd missed two calls while I was upstairs searching the other suite. The first message was from Adam.

"Hey, bud," he said. "I really liked that apartment on 11th Street. You should definitely take it. Call me."

Then I remembered. I flipped the phone closed and ran into the bedroom, where my suitcase was still sitting open on the floor of the closet. My heart sank. I reached into the pile of dirty laundry inside and pulled out the bottle of Vicodin. I had forgotten that I'd hidden them there earlier that day. Adam had planned on picking me up at the hotel that morning so we could go look at apartments. I wasn't sure if he was going to come up to my room, but I didn't want him seeing the pills—or even worse, asking for some—so I stashed them in my suitcase.

I took three Vicodin and slumped back down on the sofa. I dumped the pill bottle onto the table and started counting tablets. I wanted to know exactly how many I had left.

I took a drag from my cigarette and listened to my second voice mail.

"Hey, it's David Copperfield. I just wanted to see how you're holding up. Don't forget, you're going to be great."

ST. VINCENT'S

THE WOMAN SEATED DIRECTLY ACROSS from me wasn't wearing any underwear.

This wasn't a hunch or wishful thinking or some perverted fantasy. No, I knew she wasn't wearing any underwear because she seemed determined for me to know that she wasn't wearing any underwear. And she wasn't especially subtle. She practically hit me over the head with her vagina. This wasn't your garden-variety "Sharon Stone in *Basic Instinct* uncrossing-of-the-legs crotch shot" either. This was a full-on unobstructed view.

It was close to three A.M. on a Friday morning. We were sitting directly across from each other in an unpleasantly well-lit room at St. Vincent's Hospital. It was just the two of us. She couldn't have been older than thirty and had shoulder-length strawberry blond curls, which from where I was sitting appeared to be her natural hair color.

The room wasn't even really a room—it was more of a small alcove off to the side of the hospital's bustling triage department. She was wearing a pink paper hospital gown that she'd hiked up to her wide-open freckled thighs. To her immediate left was a counter with a small sink, a box of latex gloves, and several stacks of individually wrapped alcohol wipes. One after the next, she tore open a wipe, dropped the wrapper on the floor, and rubbed alcohol all over her face. I watched her do this dozens of times.

I didn't know where to look. I studied the worn poster illustrating the muscular system that was tacked to the wall behind her. I pretended to search for some lost item in the plastic bag they had given me to hold my clothes after I changed into my own blue paper gown. Every time I looked over at her, she was staring back at me while painstakingly wiping her face with alcohol. She looked away only in order to briefly glance down at her exposed crotch, before quickly making eye contact again.

I had zero interest in her vagina, or any vagina, for that matter. One of the many side effects of opiate abuse is the total loss of libido. And I was most definitely abusing opiates at this point. Her genitals were about as appealing to me as a Big Mac is to a vegetarian.

I'd noticed her when I first walked into the hospital about an hour earlier. She was in the waiting room, wearing ripped jeans and a low-cut black CBGB concert tee. I remember her because she laughed at me and muttered something to herself when I walked past. I can only imagine it had something to do with the fact that I was wearing a tuxedo.

I'd put on the tux earlier that evening to attend the 2001 Council of Fashion Designers of America awards gala. I'd been the editor of *Details* for about a year. The CFDA awards were presented every June and were considered by some to be the Oscars of the fashion world. Designers, supermodels, celebrities, and socialites would turn up to celebrate the year's best in womenswear, accessories, menswear, etc. Paparazzi lined Lincoln Center's grand plaza for a chance to snap a photo of Diane von Furstenberg or David Bowie and Iman or Gwyneth Paltrow or Tom Ford. It was the hottest ticket in town.

I was dreading it.

I was never terribly excited about attending events like these, but lately they'd become even less attractive. I had never been the life of the party, but I'd learned how to work a room. I usually circulated around the edges of the action, moving in only to say a quick hello when I needed to. And I was always one of the first to leave.

Still, I wasn't jaded. It was cool to be at a party with Calvin Klein and Naomi Campbell. I liked being able to double-air-kiss Karl Lagerfeld or bum a smoke from Kate Moss. I had made the cut. I was on the inside and that wasn't lost on me.

There was a perverse pleasure in walking past the assembled onlookers packed together on the sidewalk outside of these glamorous events.

"Excuse me, please," I'd say, my invitation visible in my hand as I pressed through the crowd of starstruck bystanders. "Sorry, folks. Just trying to get to the front here."

"He must be someone," I figured they were thinking as they made room for me to pass.

It was a douchebag's delight.

This night, however, I was in no mood to schmooze. In fact, I'd been anxious about it all day. When I woke up that morning, I realized that I had only a handful of Vicodin left. There were no more than thirteen pills left in the ziplock bag I kept stashed in my closet. Over the course of a year, I'd gone from taking fifteen pills a day to downing sixty. Normally I swallowed at least fifteen pills first thing in the morning, shoveling them into my mouth all at once the way some people might with a handful of popcorn at the movies. I took pride in the fact that I could get them all down with one small sip of water. I generally repeated this exercise at least four times a day.

Not on the day of the CFDA gala. I simply didn't have enough ammo. Since I wasn't scheduled to see the doctor to secure a new prescription until Monday morning at nine A.M.—the first appointment available with one of the five pain management specialists I'd been seeing—I had to make do with thirteen pills. That's all I had to get me through the weekend. It was Thursday. Of course I considered taking them all that morning, but if I had, I would have started feeling the dreaded symptoms of withdrawal by the time I was putting on my tux at around 6:30 that evening. That would have sucked. I can only imagine walking over to say hello to Tommy Hilfiger, my nose running uncontrollably as I offered a clammy handshake. Or worse, fighting to suppress the sudden urge to vomit while chatting with Helmut Lang. These were not viable options.

It was times like these that I would envy run-of-the-mill drunks. I assumed that in a pinch they could always find something to drink. It may not have been their beverage of choice. It may not have gotten them fucked up the way they needed to get fucked up, but at least it was enough to get them through. Enough to stop them from puking in front of Ralph Lauren. The way I saw it, they were lucky. Not me, no. Leave it to me to become addicted to a ridiculously expensive drug that is closely monitored by the federal government.

I had no choice but to make those thirteen Vicodin last all day. I'd deal with the hell of withdrawal in private over the weekend, just as I had countless times before. I simply needed to make it through the party. So I mapped out a strategy to do just that. I took four pills in the morning, another four at lunchtime, and four more just before leaving for the event. That left one remaining, which I carried with me in my pocket just in case I started to feel wobbly. It seemed like a solid plan.

Needless to say, by the time my taxi pulled up in front of Lincoln Center at around 7:15 P.M., I was feeling wobbly. My body was accustomed to being fed close to sixty Vicodin a day. It had little patience for anything less.

I kept it together, though. As I was walking in, Diana Ross was in front of me. I smiled as I was reminded of the time I sat directly behind her at a fashion show. When you sit behind Diana Ross, the only thing you see is Diana Ross's hair. I didn't see one model. Not one stitch of clothing. Just hair. It was one of the most memorable fashion shows I've ever been to.

As the night dragged on—these awards shows tended to move at a glacial pace—I began to feel a familiar cold sweat creeping up my spine. It was starting. My body was not only craving more drugs; it was demanding them.

I was seated with my boss, Patrick McCarthy, and a number of former colleagues from *Women's Wear Daily*. The paper's longtime fashion critic, Bridget Foley, was being honored with an award for fashion journalism, and I figured I had to stay at least until she made her acceptance speech. I was itching to leave—literally.

The upside of being addicted to pain pills is that there is no discernible evidence of use, at least not at first glance. Booze reeks. Weed stinks. Coke leaves residue around the nose and makes your jaw dance like you have a mouthful of Pop Rocks. Pills are clean and odorless and can be taken without drawing much attention to yourself. Still, I generally preferred to take them when no one was around. I excused myself from the table and went to the bathroom to take the last pill—lucky number thirteen. Maybe a small dose of the active ingredients in a single Vicodin might stave off withdrawal for another hour or so.

Leaning over the sink in the bathroom, I popped the pill and cupped a palmful of water from the faucet.

"Hello, Dan Peres."

Are you kidding me? At that exact moment, Tom Ford had to walk into the men's room? It couldn't have been a bathroom attendant or a complete stranger or another drug addict looking for privacy? This was the fashion community, for Christ's sake. Surely I wasn't the only hot mess in a tux.

Nope. It was the biggest fashion designer in the world.

"I'm just taking a Tylenol," I said, wiping the water from my mouth.

"Sure you are," he said as he walked past.

"Funny. Okay, good to see you."

That was the extent of our exchange that evening. I left shortly after returning to my seat, just as Bridget went on stage to collect her award.

My hair was damp at the temples by the time I got down to my apartment on 11th Street. My shirt was stuck to my back and my stomach was in knots. I tossed my clothes at the foot of my bed and curled up in a ball. It was happening. I'm not sure which is worse, going through withdrawal or the fear of going through withdrawal. I'd been there many times before, and I had never gotten used to it. The anxiety is crippling. It's like a scene from a horror movie. You are hiding under the bed. The boogeyman enters the room and slowly stalks around. You hold your breath. You see his feet as he goes past. You hope and pray that he doesn't find you. And just when you think he might be gone, he yanks you out by your ankles and slaughters you.

I was under the bed. He was coming for me. I was terrified.

After a couple of hours of physical misery and sheer panic, I did what anyone in that situation would do—I put on a tuxedo and went to the nearest emergency room. I wasn't ready to face the pain and was hoping for a stay of execution. Maybe I could con some exhausted resident working the graveyard shift into giving me enough pills to hold me over till Monday morning. I figured the tux might help distinguish me from every other junkie looking for a fix in the middle of the night.

"How long do you think the wait will be?" I asked the admitting nurse through a cluster of holes in the smudged glass window separating her from the crowded waiting room. "I've already had two back surgeries and I'm in agony."

What I meant to say was: "I'm in a tuxedo, in case you hadn't noticed. Clearly I should be getting some sort of preferential treatment here. I mean, look at these people. Is there a VIP check-in area or some hospital version of a first-class lounge? I didn't want to have to mention this, but I'm the editor in chief of *Details*."

"Sir, you'll have to take a seat," she said. "We'll call your name." She was chewing gum.

I was eventually moved into the brightly lit room. The woman in the pink paper gown was down to the last few alcohol wipes when a nurse came in to get me.

I picked up the bag holding my tux and followed her to an examining room. A young doctor came in a few minutes later and I took him through my standard routine. Microdiscectomy. Recurrence. Numb toes. Excruciating pain radiating down my leg. I made it a point to mention that I traveled a lot for my job as the editor of a major national magazine. This always seemed like an impressive detail.

"I'm sure you've seen it all," I told him, "but I just had the

weirdest experience. This woman and her vagina have been staring at me for the past thirty minutes. And she was rubbing alcohol
wipes on her face the entire time."

"What color gown was she wearing?" he asked as he dragged
the tip of the handle on one those knee hammers across the bottom of my right foot. "Was it pink?"

"No way! How did you know that?"

"We put the people that require psychiatric evaluation in pink
gowns. That way we can all keep an eye on them," he explained
before writing me a prescription for thirty Vicodin.

I swallowed hundreds of pills a week without giving it a second thought. It was business as usual—as normal for me as eating
three meals a day is for most people. It was only when I ran out of
pills that I realized I had a drug problem. That something needed
to change. The answer was obvious. I had to make sure I didn't
run out of pills.

The day after my emergency-room visit, I swore to myself I
would never let this happen again. It was classic morning-after
regret—the shame spiral that causes so many people to take action
on Monday mornings, like vowing to limit carbs for the rest of
the week after a big pasta dinner.

I would manage my pill intake in order to be sure I always had
a refill coming in before the old batch ran out. I could do that. Or
I could try to get larger prescriptions—more pills. That was even
better. Or I would take them every six hours instead of every four.
Maybe that was the answer. Either way, I was a smart enough guy.
I knew I could figure something out.

It was five months later when I found myself back in St. Vincent's emergency room. I'd probably gone through a few days of
withdrawal here and there at least ten times since the night of

the CFDA Awards. But this night was particularly rough. Each time the boogeyman came into the room looking for me was more brutal than the last.

It was a Tuesday. I hadn't gone to the office that day. I'd taken my last handful of pills the previous afternoon and was in full shake, rattle, and roll mode. I had a migraine, every muscle ached, and I hadn't eaten or slept in twenty-four hours. One of my doctors had given me some Valium and Ambien to help me sleep after I complained to him about increased back pain. I took two of each by nine P.M. Nothing. I popped a couple of muscle relaxers at around midnight and walked over to the hospital.

I didn't recognize the admitting nurse from my last visit. If it was the same woman, she probably wouldn't have recognized me, either. I wasn't wearing my tuxedo. Instead, I had on plaid pajama pants, a long-sleeve navy blue T-shirt with *Wu-Tang Clan* written across the chest in yellow, and a zip-front hoodie. I had never listened to the Wu-Tang Clan, but I loved the shirt and the idea that it made me appear edgier than I was. There were five or six people in the waiting room.

After making a photocopy of my insurance card, she told me it would be a few minutes before I was able to see a triage nurse.

"Is it okay if I wait outside and get some fresh air?" I asked.

"Of course. Check back with me in fifteen or twenty minutes."

I walked through the sliding glass doors and lit a cigarette—my idea of fresh air. A homeless man sitting on the wheelchair ramp that led down to the sidewalk facing Seventh Avenue asked for a Marlboro. He offered me a sip from a large McDonald's cup.

"You look like you could use some of the juice," he said after lighting his cigarette with mine. He laughed loudly. I declined.

Back inside, the triage nurse took my blood pressure and my

temperature. I ran through my usual back-pain shtick, just as I had countless times before, though it's possible I was slurring my words a bit. Sensing this, I explained that I'd been in so much pain the last few days that I hadn't managed to get too much sleep. I was sweating.

"It's warm in here," I told her. "Isn't it warm in here?"

"Why don't you go ahead and take your sweatshirt off?" she said. "In fact, why don't you go over there behind that curtain and put this on?"

She handed me a pink paper gown.

CROSSING THE LINE

CAN DOGS SMELL PILLS?

This was not a question I'd ever pondered, but for ten unbearably long minutes on an early February afternoon it was all I could think about.

I was inching toward the border in my white Ford Taurus when I spotted the dogs. I knew they could sense fear, which was already freaking me out given the fact that I was terrified, but could they actually smell Vicodin?

I wasn't expecting dogs. And now I was stuck. Fifteen lanes slowly merging into ten. There was nowhere to turn around. Nowhere to stop. I was creeping closer to the United States border inspection station that stands between Mexico and San Diego. And I had a thousand Vicodin in the trunk.

To make matters worse, I had awoken that morning with a giant pimple on the side of my nose—almost as concerning as the possibility of a Mexican prison—and I was due to be a guest on *Politically Incorrect* with Bill Maher later that day. Zits made for bad TV.

It was already 12:30 P.M. and I could still see Tijuana in my rearview mirror. I needed to be in LA by 3:00 P.M. for a quick shower and to put on my Helmut Lang suit, which was in the trunk of the rented Taurus in a gray Tumi garment bag next to a pair of shiny black Prada lace-ups and $6,000 worth of drugs.

And now I was white-knuckling my way toward California anxiously trying to gauge canine olfactory precision.

This had all seemed like a great idea just twenty-four hours earlier.

I'd walked over to the bank the previous morning. Making my way down 11th Street, I contemplated how I would travel with all of the cash I planned to withdraw. A quick internet search had informed me that if you took out $10,000 or more from a bank account, it was reported to the IRS.

I was in full "outlaw" mode, and I didn't want to tip off the feds to my movements. I'd seen *Law & Order.* This was only six months after 9/11. I knew there were "watch lists" and "persons of interest." I envisioned my name popping up on a computer screen in some nondescript federal building. "We just got word that Dan Peres has made a cash withdrawal of $10,000," they'd say. "Let's get a team in place to keep an eye on him. And take the threat level to orange."

I figured $8,000 was a safer bet.

In my mind, $8,000 in cash was something that could fill a shoe box. I thought I was going to have to tape stacks of $100 bills to my stomach the way Brad Davis did with bricks of hash in the opening scene of *Midnight Express.* Maybe I needed to pick up a roll of duct tape and a fake mustache on my way home from the bank.

It turns out that $8,000 in hundreds is no more than half an inch thick. I split the stack in two and put the money in the front pockets of my jeans. You couldn't even tell it was there.

I'd been considering doing a little shopping in Tijuana since

August, after spending a long weekend at a resort in Baja. Like many Jewish men visiting Mexico, I made a stop at a local pharmacy to pick up some Imodium and aloe. No one does diarrhea and sunburn quite like the Chosen People. While I was there, I'd bought ten OxyContin—all I could afford with the amount of cash I had on me. Still, the seed had been planted. Plus, I definitely couldn't go back to the emergency room at St. Vincent's. I was getting pills from a few different doctors, but it wasn't enough. I needed more.

When the invitation came in for me to do *Politically Incorrect*, I was excited. I loved Bill Maher and was looking forward to meeting him and possibly even getting him to do some writing for the magazine. He had taken a big hit after he called the United States "cowards" in the immediate wake of the 9/11 attacks. The show had lost advertisers and must have been struggling to bring in marquee names, which no doubt explained my invite.

I made up some nonsense to my assistant about wanting to fly to San Diego first so I could spend the night and pay my respects to a friend whose father had just died. I didn't have any friends in San Diego, but if I did, I probably wouldn't have gone out of my way to see them. Either way, someone was always sick or dying in my excuses. My addiction killed a lot of imaginary people over the years.

It took me about a half an hour to drive down to Tijuana that morning, where I'd never seen so many pharmacies in my life. They were everywhere. Huge signs touted Discount Drugs or Open 24 Hours or We Beat Any Price. There was even a guy dressed as a giant capsule with a sombrero on top, like some goofy team mascot. There were holes cut for his face and arms, and he was handing out yellow flyers promising "Lowest Drug Prices in the Country."

This was my kind of place.

Instinct told me to avoid the bigger, more polished-looking stores. I knew I was going to find what I was looking for somewhere off the main drag.

"Good morning," I said after finding a place that seemed just sketchy enough. "I'm looking for some extra-strength Vicodin or Vicodin ES."

"Do you have a prescription?" asked a man in a white lab coat.

"Nope."

He looked over toward the door before pulling a small bag out from behind the glass-top counter. It had five pills in it.

"Thirty dollars."

Aw, how cute.

"Um, yeah, I was looking for a bit more than that. A lot more, actually. Like five hundred or a thousand."

I was wearing a white button-down shirt tucked into a pair of Levi's 501s and navy low-top Chuck Taylors. I was clean-shaven and had a silver Rolex Air-King on my left wrist. A black messenger bag was slung across my chest. This guy obviously didn't know what to make of me. He shook his head and said he couldn't help me.

I spent the next forty-five minutes wandering around and striking out at every turn. If I'd been looking for large quantities of Lipitor or Viagra, I would have been set. But sadly, I didn't have high cholesterol and I had no use for an erection. Finally I stopped for a Diet Coke at small taco joint next to a gift shop. Ricky Martin's "Livin' la Vida Loca" was playing from a silver boom box next to the frozen margarita machine. The guy behind the bar was singing as he gave me my change. I decided to ask if he knew where I could get some Vicodin.

"Go to the farmacia at the end of the block on the right-hand side and ask for Izzy," he told me. "Izzy can help."

When I walked in, Izzy was smoking a cigarette behind the counter. He was built like a jockey and had a huge head of jet-black hair. I actually thought for a moment that he was wearing a fright wig. I told him what I was looking for.

"Lifetime supply?" he asked.

"I'm in a lot of pain," I explained. "Just easier to buy in bulk."

He studied me for a few seconds before asking me to follow him to a back room. The store was long and narrow and dark. The ceiling was missing a bunch of tiles and had a fan hanging down that swayed back and forth as it turned. There was a woman behind the counter helping another customer. I went with him.

"Are you DEA?" he asked once we were in the back.

"No. Definitely not. I didn't even think the DEA had any authority down here. No, man, I'm just a normal guy."

Izzy opened a rusty metal cabinet that was flush against the wall of the windowless room. They must have eaten lunch in there every day because I could practically taste the street meat and stale smoke. The cabinet door blocked my view inside. He reached in.

I just stood there quietly, my heart racing: *Please don't kill me. Please don't kill me. Please don't kill me.*

"You have cash, normal guy?" he asked as he produced a large bottle of Vicodin. I exhaled and told him that I did. He opened the bottle to show me that it was still sealed. It held five hundred tablets. He broke the seal and dropped a few into my hand so I could examine them. I'd seen bottles like this behind the counter in pharmacies in New York. He explained that it would be $3,000 for all five hundred pills. I asked if he had another one. Izzy dumped the contents of both bottles into a giant ziplock bag, nearly filling it to the top. I paid him, put the Vicodin in my bag, and headed for the car.

My heart rate had finally dropped back down to normal by the time I saw the dogs. They were on long leather leashes and were weaving in and out of the barely moving vehicles. Their handlers would touch the front tire of a car or the passenger door of a pickup truck and the dogs would give it a sniff. They were constantly moving.

I watched with fascination and terror as they got closer. What if they could smell the pills? Or worse, the fear? There was plenty of both in that Taurus. I took a quick inventory of anxieties. How would I explain being busted at the border with enough pills to choke a stable of horses? What would Si Newhouse, the owner of *Details* and my boss for the past year and a half, say? Or Patrick McCarthy, my mentor? Oy, and my poor mother. She'd be the talk of Pikesville—and for all the wrong reasons. And how about Bill Maher? This wasn't likely to get me invited back on *Politically Incorrect*. I was aware of the consequences, of course, but none of that really mattered. All that truly mattered was the drugs and making sure I had enough of them to feed what had grown into a profound habit.

I was only a few cars away from the border patrol agent who was checking IDs when one of the dogs and its handler passed in front of me. I held my breath. The air conditioner was blasting even though it couldn't have been more than 70 degrees outside. The border agent holding the leash passed by my passenger-side window and looked at me from behind his sunglasses. He stopped at the back of the car and touched the rear right tire. My heart was pounding. I held the steering wheel with both hands and watched through the side mirror. The dog darted over, its tail wagging excitedly. I was sure it was going to bark or lay down or do whatever it had been trained to do when it smelled drugs. I gripped the steering wheel tightly and held my breath.

And just like that, the dog was on to the next car.

I slowly pulled up to the border agent and handed over my driver's license.

"What was the purpose of your trip?" he asked.

"Pleasure," I said.

"Welcome home."

CHICKPEA

THE NIGHT WE MET, SHE introduced herself as Emma.

The following night she told me her name was Agnes, after her maternal grandmother, who despite being legally blind still joined her knitting circle once a week in a small town not far from Ashland, Oregon.

She would later tell me that her name was actually Mary, but that her unnaturally tanned modeling agent encouraged her to use Agnes—which was in fact her middle name—as it sounded less pedestrian.

There must have been some theory circulating in the modeling community that girls with uncommon names had an edge and booked more jobs than run-of-the-mill Susans, Beths, and Jennifers. And there may have been some truth to that. In my time at W I met a fair number of Laylas and Brees and Rileys. The same, interestingly, must have been true for male models. How else to explain the onslaught of Brocks and Holts and Palmers that made their way through the *Details* offices over the years? Porn stars and soap actors clearly subscribed to the same school of thought.

"I never tell anyone my real name," she insisted, suggesting I was special—that we had somehow developed a level of trust, a bond, a connection—that was uncommon between call girl and client. She also explained that she had only just started with the escort agency, Elegant Affairs, a week before we met at the suggestion of her roommate and fellow model, Misty. She said she'd been on only one other "call" in that time to an enormous brownstone in the West Village, and all that guy wanted to do was smoke pot and look at her feet while listening to the J. Geils Band's "Centerfold" over and over.

She was a spectacular liar. I liked that. Whatever her name was, I liked her immediately.

In the end, I didn't call her Emma or Agnes or Mary. I didn't call her anything and never had the occasion to introduce her to anyone despite spending a lot of time together. When I talked about her with Adam, we called her Chickpea—the result of one of my own inspired lies—though she never knew that.

Chickpea's face was blurred in her photos on the Elegant Affairs website. She wasn't interested in too many people knowing she was a prostitute—even an expensive one—just lonely guys like me with $1,000 to burn for an hour's worth of what the site referred to as "no-strings-attached companionship."

Just what I was looking for.

I needed to stay as far away from strings as possible. When there were strings—and there always seemed to be strings—I would have things all knotted up faster than a Boy Scout going for a merit badge.

No, I was done with strings—though it's not as if I had a choice. After being back in New York for well over a year, I had pretty much become undatable. The Kavorka—that awesome and bewildering superpower that made my time in Paris so memorable—was long gone. If anything, I had the anti-Kavorka. I'm not sure there was a name for it, but I was like a glowing chunk of kryptonite that slowly sucked the life out of anyone bold enough to spend any real time with me.

Things didn't quite turn out the way Adam and Tanner had hoped.

"Dude, you're the editor in chief of a major magazine," Tanner told me shortly after I got the *Details* job. "That's a serious panty dropper. Buckle up, brother, this is going to be a fun ride."

"I'll take that ride with you," said Adam. "I'm definitely becoming your permanent plus-one."

It was hardly the bacchanal they were expecting. But then again, I was never really a bacchanal kind of guy. And I definitely wasn't the sort of guy to lead the charge.

It didn't really matter, though. All I cared about by this point were pills. Getting them. Taking them. Obsessively counting them. I could determine at a glance how many tablets were left in those opaque orange pill bottles the same way some people tried to guess the number of candy corn in a jar on Halloween. I had a margin of error of two or three. It was a gift.

I always needed to have an accurate count—to know how many highs I had left before I would run out. Counting had become a major preoccupation.

While I was busy pursuing my pharmaceutical ambitions, there wasn't a whole lot of time for dating or hooking up or panty dropping. I did manage to stay in a relationship with my onetime plus-one, Caroline, for about ten months, though it was far from the "fun ride" Tanner predicted. This was more of a ten-car pileup on the freeway.

I'd met Caroline through one of the magazine's music writers. He brought her along to one of the *Details* staff drink outings I would throw every now and then to boost morale and show people that I was engaged. I wasn't, which I suspected was becoming obvious, but an open bar always seemed to help everyone forget.

At twenty-seven, Caroline was an A&R assistant at a small indie label, which had recently been snapped up by a global music conglomerate. From a distance you could easily mistake her for a child. She was tiny with short black hair that always looked like she had just gotten out of bed. She reminded me of a nineties-era Winona Ryder, with sharp features and pale porcelain skin and enormous glimmering eyes. And like Winona Ryder, there was something mischievous behind those dark eyes. I'd look at her one moment and see an elfin innocent with a boy's haircut and a warm smile and the next moment there'd be an intense rocker chick who didn't suffer fools gladly and may have had a switchblade in her purse. She had range.

We did a little bit of drinking and a lot of flirting at the *Details* party, which was in the darkened back room of a low-rent Irish pub not far from our midtown offices—the kind with the bar's name flickering in neon in the front window and the slightly putrid smell of steamed cabbage thick in the air. There was a pool table and a broken jukebox. Everything was sticky.

The *Details* team drank hard and fast. I, on the other hand, did not. I was a purist and didn't want to mess with my Vicodin high. I also happened to be a lightweight when it came to booze. Two drinks and the room was spinning. I generally stopped at one. Either way, I usually didn't hang around these parties long enough to get drunk. This evening I stayed mainly because I was entertained by the verbal jousting with Caroline. I'd gotten used to people laughing at my bad jokes or nodding in agreement even when I said something stupid. Perks of being the boss. Caroline was having none of it. This definitely wasn't a playful battingof-the-eyelashes flirtation. It was more of a battle of wits—a kick-him-in-the-shins-on-the-playground sort of exchange. It had a real "I'm just doing this because I'm buzzed and bored" quality to it.

We left the party and shared a taxi downtown at around midnight. I was heading home to a pile of much-needed Vicodin and she was on her way to the first of several gigs that would have kept her out till around three A.M. (I really grew to hate the word *gig*.) She leaned over to kiss me before I got out of the cab at Fifth Avenue and 11th Street. Had she not, I definitely wouldn't have, and it's likely I never would have seen her again. The kiss was sloppy—as first kisses tend to be, especially after a few drinks. I could taste stale champagne. Caroline, I would soon find out, always asked for champagne—it didn't matter if it was a dive bar, a friend's apartment, or a cramped middle seat in coach.

"I love my bubbles," she explained.

Caroline went out six nights a week. She was fiercely competitive and unapologetically ambitious. She loved meeting new people and hated cigarette smoke. We were total opposites.

We were a couple from that night on.

I should have known from the very beginning that things with Caroline were going to get messy. The first night she came to my apartment she was merciless about my taste in music. It was brutal.

"You're kidding me with this Hootie & the Blowfish, right?" she said, flipping through one of the black nylon books where I kept my CDs. "Please tell me you're fucking kidding."

I knew I should have edited out some of the lamer stuff before she came over.

"That one was sent to me for free," I said, lying.

"Indigo Girls. Melissa Etheridge," she said, laughing. "What are you, a giant lesbian?"

"All right," I said. "Wait a minute."

"Holy Christ," she yelled. "Rick Springfield? You're definitely not getting laid tonight."

"Really?" I said. "You're going to sit there and tell me that 'Jessie's Girl' isn't a classic?"

And there it was. There are those who love "Jessie's Girl" and those who don't. It's as simple as that. A mutual appreciation of won ton soup and *Frasier* reruns simply isn't enough. It would always come back to "Jessie's Girl." We were together for close to a year, but she never let it go. She loved teasing me about it, particularly in front of her Radiohead-loving, alt-rock music industry friends.

Rick Springfield aside, it wasn't all bad—at least not at first. We took a couple of great vacations, one to Barbados and another to Jamaica. She brought me home to meet her parents in suburban Atlanta, which was both eye-opening and ego-crushing.

"My dad pulled me aside just as we were leaving and told me he was really proud of me for not choosing a boyfriend based on his looks," she said to me, cracking up as we walked through the airport.

Okay, so maybe I'd put on a little weight, but this was hard to take, especially coming from her dad, who had enough hair coming out of his nose to braid.

While I never let Caroline see me swallow even one Vicodin, the addiction had grown both far more intense than the relationship and a hell of a lot more important. It was easy to hide the pills from her. I kept them buried in my laptop case in the very back of my closet and I would take them when she wasn't looking—fifteen at once with a quick sip of water. It was easy. Plus, despite being a couple, we were rarely together. She was out all the time for work, going to gigs and drinking what I can only imagine was bad champagne on the Lower East Side at places like the Mercury Lounge and Arlene's Grocery. We spent the night together once or twice a week, at best. Still, it was harder to hide the effects of pills. That would have required our never seeing each other.

"What's wrong with you?" she would ask with increasing frequency.

"I'm stressed," I would say. Or "I'm tired." Or "I don't feel well." Or—and this one really drove her nuts—"Nothing."

"What do you mean, there's nothing wrong?" she would demand, with equal parts anger and concern.

She may have been referring to the fact that I didn't want to do anything—ever. I didn't want to talk. I didn't want to go out. I didn't want to have sex.

"I've never had a boyfriend who didn't want to fuck me," she said one night, standing in front of me wearing nothing but a faded Brown University T-shirt she'd had since freshman year. "This is not normal. You are not normal."

Normal.

There was that word. It had started to come up more and more. First from Caroline. Then from my mom—"It's not normal for you to not return my call." And eventually even in my own head—"Is it normal to wake up in the middle of the night and vomit and then go back to sleep like nothing happened?"

Normal had become something of a dirty word for me. I didn't want to hear it. I didn't want to know what was normal and what wasn't.

"Normal people don't come to cocktail parties and stand in the corner," Caroline said once. "These are my friends and you barely spoke."

I figured I deserved a medal for even showing up in the first place. I rarely went out unless it was related to work, and then I was able to turn on the charm and make small talk. But when it was Caroline's friends—or my friends or my family, for that matter—I found it harder to fake it. In the end, it was just easier to not spend time with anyone. There were no questions that way. No concerns. No drama. There was no one reminding me that maybe my behavior wasn't normal.

My relationship with Caroline ultimately ended just as quickly as it had begun. She came over late one night to pick up a pair of shoes she'd left at my apartment. It was after midnight and I was sitting on the floor of my bedroom shuffling a deck of cards in front of the fireplace. The fire I'd started an hour earlier had died down but was still smoldering. The only light in the room was coming from the television, where I was watching a DVD on card magic, *Learn 40 Ways to Secretly Force a Card.*

"Pick a card," I said when she walked in the room. "This is pretty cool."

"I'm not picking a card," she said. "I'm done."

"Come on," I said. "Just one time and the I'll put them away."

"Dan, I'm done," she said. "Not with card tricks. With everything. I can't do this anymore."

I didn't put up a fight. How could I? We talked for a few minutes before she hugged me and left, shoes in hand. There were no tears in her giant eyes, only relief—like a freed hostage.

I relit the fire and shuffled the cards.

JOURNEY WAS PLAYING on the stereo the first night Chickpea came over. I had considered putting on something moodier, like Al Green or Marvin Gaye, but that seemed cheesy and somewhat cliché. I was sure that call girls had heard enough "Sexual Healing" to last a lifetime. I figured I'd give her a break. Plus, I'd recently seen an episode of *Behind the Music* on Journey and was reminded that *Raised on Radio* was the first cassette I ever bought with my own money. It may not have been a career-defining album, but it did have a couple of hits. I was an unabashed Journey fan, something the editors of *Details* took great delight in. It seemed that making fun of my taste in music was a growing obsession for many.

It had been over a month since Caroline and I broke up. I had just returned from the 2001–2002 fall/winter European men's fashion shows, with stops in Milan and Paris. I was really starting to love these trips—and not for the fashion forecasting. It was hard to get excited about shearling-lined bombers and gray flannel double-breasted suits. No, for me these trips were all about lodging. I loved the hotels. The room service. The terry cloth robes. The fact that I could luxuriate in an opiate fog in 900-thread-count Egyptian cotton sheets at the Four Seasons in Milan and the Ritz in Paris. The highs always seemed just a little bit higher in a five-star hotel.

Spending $1,000 on a call girl was the furthest thing from my mind when I walked back into the *Details*'s 34th Street offices the first Monday after my semiannual European fashion adventure. We had just shipped the all-important March issue and I needed to make sure that things were moving smoothly with April and May. I may have been something of an absentee editor—even, on occasion, when I was in the office—but I managed to focus long enough to make sure we were building a strong magazine. It mattered to me that the mix of content was right, that the images were beautiful, that the design was forward thinking, that the stories and headlines were great. This had become something of a shaky high-wire act every month. I would make it across and then look back in amazement and wonder at how I had done it—at how I was still alive.

I was on my way to lunch when Steven, an eager junior editor with a slight lisp who sat directly outside of my fourth-floor office, grabbed me and pitched a story about wealthy men ordering ultra-expensive escorts over the internet.

"These women aren't like the hooker Hugh Grant got busted with," he said, going for an older but still useful reference. "They're not streetwalkers. These are tens. Total beauties. Check it out."

I leaned over the back of his chair as he brought up the Elegant Affairs website. There was a tuna sandwich on his desk. The smell made my stomach turn. There was a grid of photos on the site's home page—*Brady Bunch* style—of women in evening gowns with their first names in bold black letters toward the bottom of each picture. Felicity. Harmony. Elle. Mia. Ebony. Emma. The whole thing reminded me of a fashion look book—catalogue-style photos of catalogue-style models, some with windblown hair courtesy, no doubt, of a blow-dryer being held just out of frame.

"Listen, I have to run," I told Steven. "Why don't you bring this up in next week's pitch meeting."

After work, I stopped by David Copperfield's apartment to check out some newly restored turn-of-the-century penny arcade games that had just been delivered and he was eager to show me. David was in New York for a couple of days—he'd been spending a lot of time on the road and at the MGM in Vegas—and he'd turned the first floor of his home into a full-blown fun house with dozens of games from the 1900s, each made of polished wood with weathered steel knobs and fixtures. We'd developed a real friendship over the course of the past year and would speak at least once a week and get together whenever he was back in New York.

I was excited to see the new penny arcade games, but I also had a present for him. When I was visiting my family in Baltimore for Thanksgiving, I found an old trick that my mother had stored in a large box in the attic with the rest of my magic stuff. It was called a Temple Screen and was made with three panels of cardboard, each around eighteen inches tall and about five inches across, which were held together with duct tape. The magician would stand the boards on a table propped up in the shape of a horseshoe and produce silk scarves from behind the screen. It was a classic. I'd also found my long black satin cape. I had forgotten I used to wear a cape when I did magic as a kid.

When I came down from the attic with the Temple Screen, I tried to throw the cape away.

"Don't do that," my mother said.

She was like the trash police. I once buried a candy wrapper in the very bottom of the trash can and she later called me into the kitchen to ask if I was the one who ate the Whatchamacallit.

"Why don't you bring the cape back to New York?" she asked. "You might want to wear it if you ever do a magic show."

"For the love of god, Mom. Leave the cape in the trash," I pleaded.

David had once told me that the first magic trick he ever bought as a kid was a Temple Screen, but he returned it after seeing how cheaply made it was. I thought he might find it funny if I gave him mine. He was actually quite touched.

I stayed at David's for about an hour. He was like a giant kid, excitedly explaining each of the arcade games before dropping a penny in and letting me play. After losing to him a couple of times in a horse-racing game that required me to crank a handle around clockwise as quickly as I could as the painted metal horse moved across the track, I had to go.

"Do you want to grab dinner?" he asked.

"I can't," I said. "I have to be at a party at eight P.M."

That was a lie. I needed to be home to get high. I'd taken my last handful of Vicodin at four P.M. and I was due for my evening feeding. *As needed for pain every 4 hours.* It was time.

Chickpea was wearing a clingy black cocktail dress with a plunging neckline in her photo on the Elegant Affairs home page. She had shoulder-length wavy blond hair. It was impossible to see her face, but I sat at the wooden desk in my small home office studying my computer screen, trying to identify features beneath the blur the same way I tried to decipher what was going on behind the Cinemax scramble when I was a kid.

I'm not sure why I did it. I wasn't horny. I rarely was those days— the Vicodin had snuffed out nearly all sexual desire. But I was transfixed. Curious. Bored. And perhaps in that moment lonesome. Or maybe I did it simply because I could. I didn't know, but I took out my American Express card and booked an appointment with Chickpea for later that night.

Steve Perry was belting out the chorus of "Be Good to Yourself" when she knocked on the door. I took a here-goes-nothing deep breath and let her in.

"Hey there, cutie," she said, giving me a big hug as if we were college friends who hadn't seen each other in years. "I'm so glad you called."

She was completely at ease.

"I'm Emma," she said, smiling. "Okay if I take my shoes off?"

She was wearing a pair of Nikes. When I booked our meeting, I had asked that she dress down. She had on a pair of tight dark jeans and a small gray cable-knit cashmere sweater that rose up to expose about an inch of her stomach when she took off her coat.

"I'm Dan," I said.

I was about to give her a fake name, but then I remembered that I'd given the escort agency my full name and credit card info, which all of a sudden seemed like a pretty stupid thing to have done. Was I in some database now? Was Elegant Affairs going to bill me for $10,000 instead of $1,000? Was I going to get arrested? Oy, my poor mother.

She took me by the hand and led me over to the sofa. The living-room fireplace was roaring. She sat Indian style facing me. Steven had been right when he said "total beauties." Chickpea was beautiful. She reminded me of Cameron Diaz from *There's Something About Mary*. She looked like the prettiest girl from small-town America—the one who tossed the baton in the Memorial Day parade. The one who played Dorothy in the local production of *The Wizard of Oz*. The one who everyone was rooting for to make it big in the big city.

Chickpea couldn't have been more than twenty-three or twenty-four. She had soft blue eyes and hadn't stopped smiling since she walked in. She was bubbly and nodded a lot whenever I said anything. The management at Elegant Affairs must have instructed the girls to ask lots of questions and make the men feel good about themselves and their accomplishments.

"You look like you're in great shape," she said. "Do you work out a lot?"

Really? I hadn't been to a gym in ages and was starting to look as bloated as a body just fished out of the East River.

"Have you read all these books?" she asked as she got up from the sofa and made her way to one of the white built-in bookcases that stretched from floor to ceiling on either side of the fireplace.

I hadn't.

"Yes," I said.

"Did you take this beautiful picture of the Eiffel Tower?" she asked, pointing to a framed black-and-white photo leaning against the bookcase.

"Karl Lagerfeld took it," I explained, trying to impress her, which seemed silly, as I was paying her to be there. She was a sure thing. Still, I wanted to be liked. And I liked feeling impressive. "Karl gave it to me as Christmas present a few years ago when I was still living in Paris," I said. "Turn it around. He wrote a message on the back."

"That's so cool," she said. "I was just there last year. My modeling agent sent me to live there for a couple of months with a few other girls."

She sat back down on the sofa, held my hand again, and asked if I minded if she smoked some pot. I didn't mind and even took a hit from the small blown-glass bowl she pulled from her purse. We talked for about forty minutes until she suggested we go into the bedroom. It was close to 12:30 A.M.

"You know what?" I said. "Do you just maybe want to hang out and get stoned and listen to music?"

"Um, sure," she said. "I need to call the agency and tell them I'm leaving. It's policy. They need to make sure I'm safe."

While Chickpea was outside on the back deck checking in with Elegant Affairs, I went to my closet to get another fifteen Vicodin. It was time. Again. When I came back from the kitchen with a glass of water, she was sitting on my bed.

"Does this fireplace work, too?" she asked. "Let's hang out in here."

I lit a fire.

She stayed till three A.M. and gave me her number before she left.

"Call me."

I did the next day. And that night she came over again. I wasn't sure if she was going to ask for $1,000, but I would have paid if she had. But she didn't. Nor did she the following night or any other night.

On Friday night of that week, Adam called at around ten P.M. and said he was in the Village and asked me to come meet him and some friends for a drink. Chickpea was over and while I was on the phone asked me to pass her the lighter.

"Who is that?" Adam asked.

"I can't really talk right now," I said. "Call me tomorrow."

He did, first thing in the morning. "Dude," he said. "Who are you hanging out with?"

I considered just telling him the truth, but didn't. I could sense that he was already worried about me. I'd been blowing him off for months, as the hold the addiction had on me tightened.

"You know that natural food store on University between 11th and 12th?" I asked. "I met her there."

I was hoping that would be enough. It wasn't.

"Go on," he said.

"We were both standing over the salad bar and I asked her if there was a difference between garbanzo beans and chick-peas. We started talking and I ended up bringing her back to my place."

It sounded like a bad script idea for some kind of vegan fetish porn. It was scary how easily I could lie to my oldest friend.

"You got laid because of a chickpea," he said. "That's awesome!"

From that moment on, whenever I would speak to Adam he would ask if I was still hanging out with Chickpea. And, more often than not, I was.

She would come over—sometimes late at night—and we would talk, smoke, watch TV, order a pizza, and occasionally have sex.

I never asked any questions. And neither did she. Neither of us had to give any excuses. Neither of us had to justify anything.

She was a pretender, just like me.

We saw each other two or three nights a week for months.

It felt normal.

TYSON

MIKE TYSON SOUNDS SO MUCH like Mike Tyson that when some-one calls you and says, "It's Mike Tyson," you think it's someone pretending to be Mike Tyson.

"Hi, Dan. It's Mike Tyson."

"Bullshit."

"What did you say?"

"Oh, sorry, Mike Tyson. Nice lisp, by the way."

"What the fuck did you just say?"

"Wait. Who is this?"

It was Mike Tyson.

He was calling to set up a time for us to meet early the follow-ing week to talk about a profile and cover shoot we were doing on him at the magazine. He told me to meet him at the corner of 118th Street and Eighth Avenue at noon on Monday and gave me his cell in case I couldn't find him.

When the time came a few days later, I couldn't.

Maybe I wrote down the wrong number, but every time I tried calling him, there was a busy signal. I must have tried a dozen times as I sat in the back of a Town Car on 118th Street. Nothing.

"I guess I'll just walk around the block and see if I can find him," I told the driver.

"Okay, if you want, but I'd stay close if . . ." he said, pausing mid-sentence. "Actually, you should be fine. I think this neighborhood isn't nearly as bad as it used to be."

I should be fine? I thought. *That's just great.*

It was far too hot to be searching the streets of Harlem for Mike Tyson, but that's precisely where I found myself on that unseasonably warm September afternoon. And to make matters worse, I was overdressed. And high. Really high. The handful of Vicodin I'd taken in the car on the way uptown kicked in around the same time I started aimlessly wandering 118th Street trying to find the former heavyweight champion of the world.

By the time I made my way down the block—past a few boarded-up storefronts, a small beauty parlor, and a garage, that, according to the sign outside, fixed flat tires "quick and cheap"—I was soaked in sweat. Two older men sat on the front stoop of one of the buildings smoking cigarettes and listening to a small portable radio. I was wearing a dark gray wool suit I'd had made in London and a silky blue knit tie. Leave it the English to make a summer suit heavier than a midshipman's pea coat. I had a gelled-up faux hawk, and despite the fact that summer had just come to an end, my skin was pasty.

Normally, I was underdressed for everything. It was my thing. I was just arrogant enough to turn up to a meeting with the CEO of a luxury goods company wearing faded jeans, sneakers, and a V-neck sweater with holes at the elbows. I liked the idea of the fashion community thinking I didn't care—that I was cool and confident enough to pull off wearing tattered Chuck Taylors to a gala dinner or a well-worn Patagonia fleece pullover in the front row at a Versace runway show in Milan.

The day of my Harlem adventure, however, I felt the need for a little extra polish. I had a print order meeting that morning where I had to present the latest issue of *Details* to Condé Nast's famously enigmatic and quirky owner, Si Newhouse, and the rest of the corporate management team. Every Condé editor in chief did this once a month, but I still got nervous for my turn. Despite having the job for a few years, I wasn't terribly confident in my relationship with Si.

My last feeding had been the night before and I knew that my body would be demanding opiates and on the verge of revolt by the time the print order meeting started at 9:30 A.M. Chickpea barely stirred when the alarm clock sounded at 8:00 A.M. She'd spent the night, as she often did at this point. Her glass bowl was on the nightstand next to her small black purse. While I never looked inside, I always imagined it held an array of condoms, a small bag of pot, and her keys.

"I don't think I've ever seen you in a suit," she said as I emerged from the walk-in closet and headed for the door. Her head was still on the pillow and her eyes were barely visible behind a mop of tousled blond hair. "You look handsome."

I felt weak. I was craving my morning feeding.

Nothing a $2,000 gray bespoke English two-piece suit couldn't fix. Either way, I couldn't show up loaded. These meetings were sobering enough sober. I would definitely have to wait until afterward to get high. This wasn't an ideal start to the day. I've never been a coffee drinker, but I imagine I needed a handful of pills in the morning the way most people needed a latte.

"Don't talk to me, I haven't had my coffee yet."

I knew the feeling.

"Why are you all dressed up?" Si asked as soon as he walked into the room. There was a large round wooden table with six chairs and a blue-and-white-striped sofa. The rubber soles of his shoes dragged against the plush carpet as he walked, making it sound like he was shuffling his feet. He was wearing a pair of tan khakis and a gray sweatshirt with *The New Yorker* printed in small black letters above his heart.

"I just felt like wearing a suit today," I said. He shrugged and sat down. I just smiled and put my hands in my pockets, which were loaded with the Vicodin I planned to take after the meeting.

These meetings tended to last less than an hour. Each page of the issue we were about to print was put into an individual plastic sleeve in a large leather book resting on an easel. I would describe the contents on each as I flipped through. Si was a quiet man, but if there was something he didn't like, he was vocal about it. We were doing some great work at *Details*. I was present just enough to see to it that we were. Still, I longed for Si's approval. It must have been obvious.

"Stay back for a second, Dan," he said after the meeting. Once everybody had left the room, he walked over and put his hands on the leather book, which sat closed on the table in front of us.

"This is great issue," he said. "You don't need to convince me of that. Stop worrying about me. I'm not your audience. Focus on making a magazine your audience wants—not one that you think I want."

It meant more to me than he'd ever know.

He walked out of the room, his shoes rubbing the carpet as he went.

"EXCUSE ME. WOULD you by any chance know where I could find Mike Tyson?" On my second trip down 118th Street, I decided to stop and ask the men on the stoop if they could help me.

"Follow the birds," one of the men told me.

It felt like some kind of riddle. Like a *Raiders of the Lost Ark* clue. Was this code? *Maybe they were protecting his privacy*, I thought, like I'd heard the residents of Cornish, New Hampshire, used to do when some outsider came to town and asked for J. D. Salinger.

"I'm sorry," I said. "I don't understand."

"The pigeons, son," he said, pointing above my head. "He's up there on the roof with the pigeons."

I crossed the street and stood in front of what appeared to be a derelict redbrick building that looked as if it was being held together by the wrought-iron fire escape zigzagging along its facade like a rusty zipper. I could hear the collective flutter of the birds flying overhead.

"Hello!" I yelled toward the roof, six stories above the sidewalk. "Hello! Anyone up there?"

After I called up a few more times, someone came to the ledge. "Dan, is that you?" It was Tyson.

I squinted into the blazing sun, trying to zero in on the source of the famously high-pitched voice above. A feathery cyclone of pigeons whirled over his head like some Hitchcockian nightmare. It was mesmerizing. Hypnotic, almost. It made me dizzy.

"Yes," I called back. "Where do I go? How do I get up there?"

He didn't respond. I figured maybe he didn't hear me.

"How do I get up there?" I shouted once more.

From where I was standing, it appeared that Tyson was dangerously close to the edge of the roof. It took everything I had to stop myself from yelling, "Hey, Mike Tyson, please be careful or you might get hurt."

Tyson, meanwhile, thought it might be a good idea to welcome me to the neighborhood. "Look, everyone," he yelled from the roof, "there's a white man up here."

Maybe this was payback for the whole "nice lisp" thing. I'd read somewhere that he got his start fighting when he was a boy by beating up neighborhood kids who made fun of his voice.

"Very funny," I said.

He's just fucking with me, right? I thought.

The fifteen Vicodin I'd taken in the car were now in full effect. I was feeling no pain, and for a brief moment began to wonder if I could actually take a punch from Mike Tyson.

"Don't be such a pussy," he said. "I'm sending Jimmy to get you."

I'm not sure if it was the heat or the pills or both, but by the time the door to the building was flung open a few minutes later, I was swaying back and forth like a rabbinical student at the Wailing Wall. The man standing in front of me appeared as run-down as the building he just stepped out of. He was missing a few important teeth and was rail-thin—his *Just Do It* Nike T-shirt was huge and hung on his frame like a sheet on a clothesline. We stood there studying each other.

Yo, Mike, there's a junkie down here on the sidewalk, man, I thought about yelling toward the roof.

"You Dan?" the man asked. It was Jimmy. "Let's go."

He didn't speak much as we slowly climbed six flights of alarmingly creaky stairs. It was hot and dark, and I was sure that one of my size 11, shiny black cap-toe Church's shoes was going to bust right through one of the stairs and I was going to plunge into the building's basement.

This isn't going to end well, I thought. *What am I doing here?*

I was there at the suggestion of Tyson's publicist. She called me a few weeks before to ask me if I wouldn't mind meeting Mike in person and spending some time with him.

"I think it would be good for him," she said. "He needs a pos-

itive influence in his life. He had a great relationship with John
Kennedy Jr., and I think he needs people like that around him.
Someone like you."

Done.

Nothing fluffs a fragile ego quite like being compared to John
Kennedy Jr. I'd been bullshitting everyone for years at this point.
Surely I could convince a train wreck like Mike Tyson that I was a
stable and guiding presence.

Light poured in from the open door as Jimmy and I made our
way up the final flight of stairs. The entire roof was a Jackson
Pollock canvas of bird shit. There was a coop built of plywood and
chicken wire toward the center. Tyson was wearing shorts and a
white T-shirt. He was heavier than I thought he'd be, but who was
I to judge—I'd been bulking up a bit myself. I walked over to say
hello. He smiled as he came toward me.

The last time I'd seen Mike Tyson in person, he wasn't smiling.
It was the summer of 1989. I was seventeen and about to head off
for my freshman year at NYU, when I saw him fight Carl "The
Truth" Williams in Atlantic City. It was the first time I'd ever been
to a professional fight. My stepfather, Jerry, got tickets and took
the whole family. It was like nothing I'd ever seen before.

The fight was held in Boardwalk Hall just next to the Trump
Hotel where we were staying. I felt like an extra in a big Hollywood production. There were tan fat men in tuxedoes chomping
on cigars, with bosomy women in shimmering slinky dresses on
their arms. There was a man walking around talking on a cell
phone—I'd only ever seen one in a movie—the size of a baguette.
LeRoy Neiman, with his giant mustache and slicked-backed hair,
was up front talking to a guy in a fedora. Don King was there.
So was Donald Trump. Both men easily identifiable from twenty
rows back by their hair.

When I went to the bathroom before the fight, Jesse Jackson was at the urinal next to me. Basic urinal etiquette, while unwritten, is clear. You don't talk to the guy next to you while you're peeing. Even if you have known the guy next to you your entire life, you don't talk to him. Even if he's a civil rights icon—especially if he's a civil rights icon. It's a simple but very important rule and one that I broke that night.

"How's it going?" I said, making a point to keep my eyes forward. Eye contact at the urinal was also generally frowned upon.

"Hello," Jesse Jackson said.

"Just wanted to let you know that I'm a big fan," I told him.

"I appreciate that," he said before flushing and walking away.

To this day, every time I see Jesse Jackson on the news, no matter what he's saying or which cause he's championing, I turn to the person next to me and say, "I peed next to him once."

The energy in the arena that night was like nothing I'd ever experienced, and it got even more intense when the fighters made their way to the ring. We were in the seventh or eighth row of the risers directly behind the floor seats. My seat was next to the aisle, which meant that as Tyson made his way from the locker room to the ring, he came right past me. There was a crush of people around him—police, trainers, men in suits. Public Enemy's "Fight the Power" was blaring. Tyson had on black trunks and black boots and wore a white towel with the center cut out of it like a poncho. He was lean and he had an intense, distant look in his eyes as he walked past. He went on to knock Williams out in the first round. A single left hook and down he went. Dazed, Williams made it to his feet, but the referee waved his arms and called the fight. It was over.

This was Tyson at his peak—before the rape conviction and

jail. Before Holyfield's ear and bankruptcy. Before the face tattoo. By the time I met him, he was nearing the end of his career. The appeal of a Tyson fight, much like the man himself, was in decline. He hadn't held a heavyweight title in years, but he was a powerful, albeit polarizing, cultural figure desperately in need of redemption. I loved second acts and was excited to put him on the cover.

Tyson was scheduled to fight Clifford Etienne in New Orleans at the end of the year and was in New York training and, on at least one oppressively hot September afternoon, hanging out with his pigeons on a Harlem rooftop.

Birds circling overhead, I reached out to shake his hand, which was softer than I had expected. He didn't let go, instead tugging me in for a bro hug I wasn't prepared for and completely botched.

"You like pigeons?" he asked me.

I chose not to tell him that I'd eaten one once. I was living in Paris and a friend of mine connected me with the chef, Éric Ripert, who was in town for a few days. Eric took me to dinner at Alain Ducasse, where I'm pretty sure they brought us the entire menu, including a pigeon sliced in half lengthwise. Eric sat across the table from me and insisted that I have a taste of the brain.

"They are incredibly smart birds," said Tyson.

"I'm sure," I said.

From the roof you could see miles in every direction. Weather-beaten water tanks tagged with graffiti stood sentry atop neighboring buildings. We stood there talking, necks craned toward the sun as his birds flapped overhead.

Tyson was surprisingly self-aware and introspective. He talked about people thinking he was a thug and a rapist and maintained he was a different man now, not the greedy, impatient, and immature young man he once was. He mentioned his late manager Cus

D'Amato more than once and asked thoughtful questions about me and the magazine, but the weightier the conversation got, the heavier my head felt. After about forty-five minutes, I couldn't look up at the pigeons anymore. I couldn't hold my head up straight.

There was no escaping the heat, yet somehow Tyson didn't have a bead of sweat on him. I, meanwhile, looked like Albert Brooks in *Broadcast News*. I peeled my jacket off. My shirt was completely soaked. I was dizzy and started to teeter. I looked at Tyson standing in front of me and tried to steady myself. He was a blur. This is what Carl "The Truth" Williams must have felt like that night in Atlantic City back in 1989.

I took a deep breath and bent my knees. I remember watching an episode of *America's Funniest Home Videos* with a bunch of guys I knew when I was in college. Bob Saget introduced a whole segment on grooms passing out at the altar during their weddings. "You got to bend your knees," said Aaron Lefkowitz. "My mom's a wedding planner. It's all in the knees." Lefkowitz spat when he talked, so I did my best to avoid conversation with him, but I always remembered the knee thing. It came in handy on more than one occasion.

"I think I should probably get going," I told Tyson. "I need to get back to the office."

We shook hands and bro-hugged. Botched again.

"Jimmy will take you down," he said.

The stairway seemed even hotter and narrower on the way down. Twenty stairs. Turn. Twenty stairs. Turn. Twenty stairs. Turn. It was unending. It felt like I was in an M. C. Escher poster. Twenty stairs. Turn. Twenty stairs. Turn.

I finally stumbled onto the sidewalk like a drunk from a dive bar. My Town Car was sitting right there. I walked behind the

Lincoln, bent down, my arm resting on the trunk, and vomited on 118th Street.

Jimmy was standing in the doorway looking at me when I stood up.

Yo, Mike, there's a junkie down here on the sidewalk, man.

ROCK STAR

THE ROCK STAR WORE NAIL polish.

It was a deep dark red. Almost black. You could see it on the poster Adam had tacked to the wall of his childhood bedroom, where the five band members stood shoulder to shoulder, one head of hair bigger than the next. (This was the eighties, and the Pikesville girls wore their hair the exact same way—bangs, voluminous teased-out curls, crispy to the touch.)

In the poster, which hung just above the shelf that housed Adam's impressive collection of colognes, the lead singer wore sunglasses and had his hands in the pockets of a black leather vest, which hung open, showing off his bare chest and a few long necklaces. Four of the band members were wearing painted-on leather pants—the drummer's had fringe running down the side of each leg. Not the rock star. He was wearing a pair of faded skintight jeans, a white T-shirt, and an equally faded denim jacket. He was the only one with an instrument—his famous red and white guitar held upside down, the body clutched tightly against his chest with the neck pointing down toward his well-worn ankle-high black boots. He was also the only one wearing nail polish.

Even though he wasn't the front man, the rock star was the *man*. He was the one Kurt Loder interviewed on *The Week in Rock*. He was the one in the center of the poster. And he was the one Adam and Robbie used to take turns imitating back in the eighties when they would crank the band's live album in Adam's bedroom, one jamming on air guitar and the other using a black vent brush as a microphone. They would put on full concerts right there in Adam's bedroom—dropping to their knees for blistering guitar solos and strutting around the room clutching the mic with all the confidence and camp of David Lee Roth. Most of the time, I would just watch. The perennial spectator. An audience of one in an imaginary arena somewhere in the Midwest or Eastern Europe or wherever Adam decided they were.

Occasionally I would join in. "Why don't you play keyboard, my brother?" Robbie said. I liked being called "brother." It made me feel like one of the guys. But—rather like keyboard players in eighties hair bands—I was like the fifth guy in a group of friends, easily replaced without anyone really noticing. The guy who was just psyched to be included on the poster in the first place. I wasn't a core member. I wasn't essential to the DNA of the group.

Playing air piano requires a lot of commitment—far more than I could muster. Plus, the keyboard player was always off to the side and was seldom the focus of the music videos we watched. It was challenging to find a solid reference on which to base my performance, so I copied the only piano player I could think of and wound up swaying from side to side with my eyes closed as we played a sold-out stadium in Detroit. "Jesus, you look like Stevie Wonder," Adam said, interrupting an especially spirited jam.

I was a great pretender, of course. In fact, I can't remember a time when I wasn't pretending. But my pretending was born of necessity—first as an escape and then ultimately as a matter of survival. Pretending to be a rock star in front of Robbie and Adam was theater, and this is where I came up short. I felt like a phony.

The rock star wasn't wearing nail polish the night we met. I checked when he handed me a rolled-up $20 bill in the back of his limo. Maybe nail polish was an eighties thing. This was the new millennium, after all. His hair was shorter and it's doubtful he could've still squeezed into the same faded jeans from the poster, but he looked surprisingly good for a guy who, at least according to the entertainment shows, had been in and out of rehab a bunch of times and was on his third divorce. We had just left the Chateau Marmont and were making our way west on Sunset. It was nearly midnight, and the yellow Tower Records sign was still aglow. I took the rolled-up bill and snorted a toothpick-sized line of a crushed 80-milligram OxyContin pill off the cover of the *Details* issue I'd come to LA to celebrate with a party at the Chateau.

Hosting these events came with the job. We threw them a few times a year to celebrate some movie star or a special section we'd put together. This was where *my* kind of pretending saved me. Of course I would have preferred to have been holed up in my hotel room or in my apartment back in New York shrouded in a cloud of cigarette smoke, a few pills away from oblivion or worse. That was my comfort zone. Yet I managed to work the room with ease, make speeches or toasts even, and laugh with celebrities and fashion designers about things that were neither memorable nor funny. This was pretending and I was a rock star.

The party that night was packed with Hollywood stars. I think Lindsay Lohan was there. Shia LeBeouf may have been, too. It's hard to say. The people of Los Angeles—or at least the ones who turned up at parties like this—had perfected the art of looking like someone. It's as if central casting showed up, had a few mojitos, and then puked "types" all over the place. There were *agent types* mingling with *model types* flirting with *producer types* talking shop with *rocker types*. And of course there were the *actor types*. So it could have easily been Shia LeBeouf, but it may also have been one of several dozen *leather-cuff-wearing, beanie-topped, American Spirit–smoking types* who helped fill out the room on nights like this. The only way for me to really know for sure that someone was actually *someone* was when Kristin, the magazine's publicist, came bouncing over to tell me in her singsongy voice that she needed me to pose for a picture with "this one" or "that one."

I dreaded these photo ops. That's what Kristen called them, and it always made me think of events far more official—like the time George W. Bush moseyed across the deck of a destroyer in a flight suit like an extra in a poorly cast remake of *Top Gun*. Pictures of me with celebrities hardly mattered, and I resisted as often and as aggressively as I could. *Details* had taken over a portion of the Chateau's iconic Spanish Gothic lobby, and whenever I spotted Kristin making her way over, I would duck into one of the room's massive arched windows and try to disappear in the drapes.

I hated the way I looked in pictures, especially when I was standing awkwardly next to a chiseled Hollywood actor with golden skin, an artfully tousled bed head, and a blinding Chiclet smile. I was pasty and doughy and brimming with self-doubt. Plus, I was easily twenty-five pounds overweight and my chest had ballooned to what felt like a set of B-cup man boobs that always ended up looking like D cups in photos. Then there were my teeth. I never liked my teeth, even after two years of braces and several costly whitenings. I'd been smiling with my mouth closed since I was a kid. And my hair . . . Oy. A thinning fauxhawk reinforced with enough product to style a boy band. So these photo ops—me side by side with the superhero from the superhero movie—made me feel like the poor schmuck in a plastic surgeon's "Before" photo. I would eventually end up giving in to Kristin's requests and stand still—lips pursed and turned slightly downward like a pensive Bill Clinton—long enough for the photographer to fire off a few shots. I struggled to produce my usual half-smile the night of the party at the Chateau.

I was irritable and distracted and anxious. I was also nervous. I'd made the decision about an hour before the party that I was going to try heroin. That I needed to try heroin. Heroin and opiates were pretty much the same, or so I'd been told. It was time. I was ready. I'd considered this a couple of times before when I'd run out of pills, but had never had the courage to go through with it. After all, heroin was a drug. A real drug. A dirty drug. A druggie's drug. Pills were clean. Prescribed and dispensed by learned men and women in white lab coats with framed degrees hanging over their desks. Pills came in tamper-proof bottles and had warning labels. Labels I completely disregarded, but still. They seemed safe. Kids from Pikesville didn't do heroin. Kids from Pikesville went to summer camp. Kids from Pikesville knew the difference between lox and nova. They played tennis at the club. They married other kids from Pikesville and made their own kids from Pikesville.

I'd spent two hours earlier in the day at a neurologist's office in Sherman Oaks trying to get a prescription and came away empty-handed. I tried calling at least eight doctors in and around Beverly Hills, sitting Indian style on the floor of my beige hotel room at L'Ermitage crossing off names in the yellow pages as I went, but no one was willing to give a same-day appointment to a new patient—let alone one from out of town. I was convinced that every receptionist was on to me. That they were discussing me in a chat room—tipping each other off about the yuppie junkie from New York.

I ended up in the Valley.

It had been twelve hours since my last high, which wiped out my stash, and I was feeling the familiar pangs of desperation. My addiction had progressed to the point where I was no longer taking a set number of pills every day, which made it impossible to determine when exactly I might run out. Sometimes swallowing sixteen at a time took me where I needed to go. Other times it was eighteen. And still others it was twenty-one. Addiction is not an exact science. I was feeding a beast and it was always hungry.

To make matters worse, Vicodin wasn't getting me over the finish line anymore. I'd recently switched to something stronger. I had graduated from 7.5-milligram extra-strength Vicodin to 15-milligram tablets of Roxicodone. They were twice as strong and, I was sure, much healthier to abuse.

Here's my thinking: One of the active ingredients in extra-strength Vicodin is acetaminophen (Tylenol). So basically, I'd been putting somewhere in the neighborhood of sixty Extra Strength Tylenol tablets in my body every day for years. That's more than two of the small bottles sold in the pain relief aisle at Rite Aid—a day. Roxies were made up of just the opiate. No acetaminophen. It was the perfect drug.

And it was Roxies that I was looking for when I took a car service to the doctor's office in the Valley that spring afternoon. I don't recall it being particularly hot outside, but the office was freezing.

"Our air conditioning is broken," the woman behind the desk explained when I asked why it was so cold. I was shivering. Like many doctor's receptionists I'd met—and there had been quite a few—she was as chilly as the waiting room. They were universally unfriendly, for some reason, which drove me nuts, as I also had an addiction to being well liked.

"Fill this out," she said, thrusting a clipboard toward me without looking up.

Thankfully, the doctor was warmer. He had a port-wine stain just below his left eye, which I couldn't stop staring at. He was chatty and had actually done his residency in Baltimore at the hospital where I was born. This was a gift. It gave me a chance to win him over—a reason for him to do me a favor. We had Baltimore in common. What were the odds? I tried everything. The Orioles. John Waters. Crabs. I cranked up the charm. I explained that I'd been treated on and off in New York for lower back pain and that Roxicodone usually helped. He wasn't having it. Not without an MRI, he told me. Dr. Do-right wasn't budging. In the end, he gave me a small prescription for Soma, a muscle relaxer, and told me to follow up with my doctor when I got back to New York. No amount of Soma was going to give me what I needed. I dropped the script in a trash can in the parking lot and climbed into the waiting Town Car.

My mind was made up. Fuck it—I was going to do heroin. No MRI required. No icy receptionist. No hassle. I would do only a little. I'd snort it. Enough to get rid of the chills and the headache and the cramping that were on the way. Enough to get me high, but not so much as to fuck me up. Or kill me. It would be like a Band-Aid—something to hold me together until I returned to New York three days later. A temporary fix.

On the way back to the hotel, I told my driver that the magazine I worked for was doing a story on celebrities and drugs and that after the party I was considering taking a look at some of the areas in town where the rich and famous might go to score. It sounded like such bullshit. An obvious lie. I don't know why I cared, but it was important to me that the driver think I was a good guy. I was usually much more confident in my lies. I needed to be—there were so many of them.

"Huge problem out here," he said. "So many lives and careers ruined."

He seemed to know a lot about the subject and told me about the intersection of Western and Melrose. And Skid Row. More options on Skid Row, he said. He then, without missing a beat, proceeded to explain that he was a former addict and that the Church of Scientology's drug program, Narconon, had saved his life. He recommended speaking to some of the counselors he worked with for the magazine article we were doing. I assured him we would.

I saw the rock star talking to a few people just outside of the Chateau Marmont's main entrance when I snuck away from the *Details* party for a cigarette and a minute to myself. He wasn't there for our event. If he had been, Kristin surely would have shoved me into a picture with him by that point. Four or five women in their mid-twenties stood a few feet to his right, smoking and laughing just loud enough to try and get his attention. Every few seconds one of them would glance over to see if he had noticed her. He hadn't. The laughs grew louder. Still nothing. One of them asked his friend for a light. The rock star didn't even look up. It was as if they weren't there. Women like this—beautiful and braless— had been trying to catch his eye for decades. He didn't need to see them. He'd seen them. If he wanted one, he knew where to look. And—I suspected as I studied the scene—one look was all it would have taken.

It had probably been that way for twenty-five years. His band was a constant on MTV back in the early days, and they had reached icon status by the time I was in college, where a guy who lived down the hall from me once went to three nights' worth of back-to-back sold-out shows at the Garden. I hadn't listened to the music in ages, but if one of their power ballads came on while I was in the car, I would crank it up and—if I was alone—sing mangled lyrics at the top of my lungs. By the time I ended up in the back of the limo with him, the band hadn't had a hit in well over a decade or even put out a new album, for that matter. But they were still touring, and their old concert T-shirts had become trendy vintage shop finds worn ironically by hot chicks with cut-off jeans and cowboy boots.

I watched the women watch the rock star for another couple of minutes before stubbing my cigarette out in a crowded ashtray. As I turned to head back to the party inside, the rock star looked me dead in the eyes. "This guy right here?" he asked one of his friends.

I flashed my non-smile smile, as if to say *Sorry for creeping you out*, and headed toward the door.

"Dan, is that you?"

It was Lila. I'd been so busy watching these women pretend not to notice the rock star that I failed to notice that Lila was standing right next to him. Of course Lila knew him—she'd always had a way of finding herself in the center of the action. It was her gift and what made her a great publicist.

I met Lila shortly after I started at *WWD* in the early nineties when I was an associate editor covering parties for the Eye page and she was a junior fashion publicist for a showroom on Seventh Avenue. Despite being total opposites—me with my chinos and Brooks Brothers button-downs and brown bucks and Lila with her tattoos and fishnets and fedoras—we became friends. If I was assigned to cover three parties on any given night, odds were that I'd run into Lila at two of them. She was perfect for LA and moved there to start her own business repping West Coast fashion brands around the same time I came back from Paris.

She ran over and gave me a hug. "I can't believe you're still smoking," she said. "You never looked like a smoker to me."

Do I look like someone who does heroin? I thought to myself. *'Cause I'm about to go get some.*

"Come meet my friends," she insisted. "Do you know [the rock star]?"

Lila explained that the rock star was considering launching a fashion line and that we should definitely speak. She told him that I was a men's fashion expert and that he shouldn't do anything without first hearing what I thought. She had always been prone to hyperbole. One look at me, and this guy would have been able to tell that I was hardly a fashion maven. I was basically wearing the same thing I was wearing when I first met Lila a dozen years ago, only more expensive versions.

"Why don't you join us for dinner?" asked the rock star. "We're about to sit down."

It wasn't unusual for me to be introduced to celebrities who were thinking about getting into fashion. Over the years, I'd had countless conversations with singers or models or NBA All-Stars who were interested in starting brands. The rock star wanted to put together a small collection of leather accessories for men and then eventually get into clothing. These projects seldom—if ever—got off the ground. No one wanted to buy a belt from an aging rocker. They were barely buying them from aging designers. I didn't say that, of course. Instead, I explained that I couldn't leave my party yet and that I would come by in an hour for a drink.

The final stragglers left the party at around eleven P.M., not long after they shut down the open bar. I was feeling pretty good, especially considering the fact that I should have started feeling signs of withdrawal already. It's amazing, but the promise of a high was able keep the boogeyman at bay—at least for a few hours. I was going to get heroin, and even though I was sweating a bit and had a slight headache, I was holding it together nicely.

The rock star, Lila, and two men were sitting at a table in the Chateau's restaurant when I stopped by to say good night. The other men looked like musicians, but because this was LA, they probably weren't. They both had arms covered in tattoos and were wearing an unnecessary amount of silver—rings on nearly every finger and heavy stacks of bracelets on each wrist. Had it not been for the fact that one of them was bald and the other had shoulder-length hair, it would have been difficult to tell them apart. I'd never been a big fan of men wearing jewelry. Obviously certain guys could pull it off—Johnny Depp, Run-DMC, the pope—but wearing an entire jewelry store was something else altogether. Ed Hardy was created for guys just like this.

The rock star waved me over as I walked toward their table, and Lila jumped up to give me another big hug.

"Do you want something to drink?" he asked.

"I'd love a Diet Coke," I said.

"Come on, I haven't seen you in forever . . . have a drink with me," Lila demanded.

"You know, I have a little headache and Diet Coke always seems do the trick," I said.

"I think I have some Tylenol in my bag," she said, reaching for an overstuffed black leather purse.

"No," I said, putting up both of my hands as if to stop oncoming traffic. "I'm good."

I did have a headache, of course, but I also didn't want to drink any alcohol, as I wasn't sure that I should be mixing booze and heroin on my first outing. I was a cautious druggie. An oxymoron if ever there was one.

My plan was to join them long enough to finish my soda. My

stomach was turning—equal parts withdrawal and nervousness about my late-night plans. It was a perfect Southern California night—clear skies and just cool enough to keep the sweat from beading up on my upper lip and showing through my shirt. This was a plus—the perspiration could get pretty bad during the first few hours of withdrawal, and I didn't want to sit there making small talk while sweating like Nixon.

Most of the tables on the terrace were still full. The rock star was wearing black—jeans, a denim jacket, and a long-sleeve Henley unbuttoned down to the middle of his chest. I'm not sure why, but I was expecting him to be aloof—maybe even a little bit of a dick. He always looked so intense in the music videos. Angry, even. But he wasn't a dick. He was charming and asked a bunch of questions about me and the magazine and men's fashion. And he was funny. You don't expect rock stars to be funny. He laughed a lot. He laughed the laugh of a two-pack-a-day smoker.

"How's your back, by the way?" asked Lila. "The last time I saw you before you moved to Paris you came to a meeting in my office and ended up lying on the floor. I felt so bad for you."

I'd been faking back pain for so long at this point that it was oddly refreshing to be reminded that it was once real.

"Comes and goes," I said. "It's much better than it was back then, but it still hurts sometimes. Like today."

"You take oxy for that?" asked the rock star.

A question only an addict would ask. I was really starting to like this guy.

"Whatever does the trick," I said.

I explained that I took oxy or Vicodin or Roxicodone, but that I didn't bring any medicine with me from New York, so I should probably head back to L'Ermitage and get some rest. I had a car waiting, I told them, and I didn't want to keep the driver too long.

"Call him and let him go," said the rock star. "I'll give you a ride to your hotel. I have something in the car that might take care of that back pain."

Addicts have the strange ability to sense when someone else is an addict—kind of like vampires knowing when someone else isn't human. I wasn't human. It must have been obvious to him.

The back of the limo smelled like smoke. The rock star had left a small leather bag that looked like a fanny pack in the corner of the car's L-shaped leather sofa. Bluish-white LED lights illuminated a two-foot-long curved rosewood bar on the opposite side of the car, next to the door we just climbed through, where two beveled glass decanters, one with Scotch and the other with vodka, sat in recessed holders on top next to an ice bucket. Backlit champagne glasses hung underneath like icicles. And of course there was wall-to-wall carpeting. It felt like the inside of a brothel. I'd been taught from my earliest days as a reporter at *Women's Wear Daily* that stretch limos were the height of tacky—right up there with walking through a party with a lit cigarette in your hand or grown men wearing shorts in the evening. I could practically hear Robin Leach— champagne wishes and chlamydia dreams.

"Billy, this is Dan," the rock star said to the limo driver through the open partition. "He needs to go to L'Ermitage. Easier to drop me first?"

Billy said that it was and slowly pulled away from the hotel. The melting ice on the bar sloshed as we turned onto Sunset and the rock star unzipped his fanny pack and took out a small round plastic container the size of a Carmex lip balm jar. He dumped the contents of the container onto the *Details* issue he grabbed from a stack in the hotel lobby—Kristin made sure they were there— and separated the pile into four lines with a matchbook cover.

I'd never snorted oxy before. I took the rolled-up $20 bill, leaned down, and went for it. As I inhaled, I suddenly became very aware that my pinkie was extended like I was sipping an imaginary cup of tea in some kid's playroom. I must have looked ridiculous. Other than smoking an occasional joint, I hadn't done drugs with anyone in years. I wasn't a social user.

The rock star didn't extend his pinkie.

We pulled up to his house somewhere behind the Beverly Hills Hotel, and Billy punched a code on a keypad that opened a white wooden gate. It was a single-level modern house with floor-to-ceiling windows. As we made our way to the top of a circular driveway he told me who used to live there, but I had no clue who he was talking about. I said, "Cool," and nodded. Houses in LA had pedigree.

"Great hanging with you, man," the rock star said as he opened the door. "Let's stay in touch."

"Definitely," I said. "Would it be okay if I made a quick stop on the way to my hotel?"

"Billy, take him wherever he needs to go," he said.

He went in for a bro hug, which I botched just as thoroughly as I had with Tyson, and we said good night.

"Do you know where Skid Row is, by any chance?" I asked Billy as he pulled out of the rock star's driveway.

"The band?" he asked, giving me a quick glance over his right shoulder as he made his way toward Santa Monica Boulevard along the quiet streets of Beverly Hills.

I fed him the same bullshit I gave to my driver earlier in the day about celebrities and drugs and a magazine article. It still felt like a lie. He told me he knew exactly where to take me.

"That's Dr. Phil's house," he said as we rolled past a well-lit gated property somewhere below Sunset. It was after midnight and a full moon hung in the sky like a giant Klieg light there to simulate a full moon. Dr. and Mrs. Phil would have been fast asleep. That's what normal people did, I told myself. Normal people slept at night. They woke up early. They went running. Or to the gym. Normal people had routines. Normal people lived their lives. I was desperate to be normal.

But I wasn't.

Billy told me that he worked for a limo service out of La Jolla and that he drove the rock star whenever he attended an event. They'd been to a gallery opening earlier in the evening before having dinner at the Chateau. It was a last-minute booking and all the company had for him to take was the stretch. He preferred an SUV. So did the rock star. Though he had a full head of gray hair, Billy was only in his mid-forties. "Fucking divorce," he said.

I eventually started feeling the effects of the oxy. I kept breathing in through my nose the way my doctor asked me to when he held a stethoscope to my back. Slow, deep breaths. I wanted to be sure everything I snorted had made its way into my bloodstream. It definitely wasn't enough to get me high, but my headache was gone and I felt a slight tingling just behind my eyes. I was relaxed for the first time all day.

Billy eventually pulled the limo over the curb. I had no idea where we were or how long we'd been driving. We'd been talking more or less the entire way—or more specifically, Billy had been talking. He was a sharer. I sat in the back, at the end of the L-shaped seat closest to the partition, smoking cigarettes and listening. His ex-wife used to have the body of a pinup, but had put on a ton of weight since their divorce, which brought him endless joy. He saw his daughter only about once a week—and usually for breakfast—because his work schedule was so unpredictable.

He listened to books on tape during his frequent late-night drives back down toward San Diego and had recently been making his way through a bunch of Michael Connelly thrillers.

"How's this?" he asked, putting the car in park and turning in his seat to face me.

If it was Skid Row, it wasn't anything like I'd imagined. I was expecting a tent city. People with stained blankets and matted hair huddled in rows on the sidewalk like the teenage girls I'd seen on the news lining up overnight to buy *NSYNC tickets. People pushing shopping carts loaded with fraying plastic bags and mangy dogs. The great unwashed masses. There wasn't any of that. Still, it felt a million miles away from Beverly Hills, and I was relieved when Billy locked the doors.

Across the street, a man in is early twenties sat on a too-small dirt bike in front of an empty parking lot. He looked at the limo, took a sip from the can he was holding, and rode off down a dark side street. I told Billy I was going to take a look around and that I shouldn't be too long.

"Are you sure?" he asked. "Maybe you should do your sight-seeing from the car."

"I'll be fine," I told him. "I won't be long."

I got out of the car—fueled by adrenaline and desperation—and walked around the corner in the same direction as the guy on the bike. On my right, a row of two-story buildings ran all the way to the next street corner. Most of the stores on the street had black metal folding gates covering large plate-glass windows. Many were boarded up. The awnings hanging over doorways were faded and torn. "Discount Furniture," read one. There was a large FOR LEASE sign in one storefront. "Prime Hollywood Location," it said above a broker's name and phone number. I must have been in Hollywood, but there was nothing "prime" about this location.

The guy on the bike was talking to someone about a half a block away from where I stood. When he saw me, he slowly rode over. He was holding a can of Dr Pepper. I just stood there. I was tempted to walk over and shake his hand but thought better of it.

It's never a good idea to show up in a stretch limo wearing designer khakis and blue Italian suede slip-ons when looking to score dope in the middle of the night on a sketchy street corner. I was dressed like a vacationing aristocrat. I looked like I should have been carrying shopping bags on the streets of Saint-Tropez. I'm not sure I knew what my element was, but it was pretty clear that I was out of it. But that's how it happened the first—and only—time I ever tried to get heroin.

"You lost?" the guy on the bike asked as he rode past before turning around and stopping just in front of me. He was wearing red sweat pants and a red Nike shirt. Tonal dressing was all over the runways in Milan last season, but I chose not to share that.

"I'm looking for some H," I told him. My voice quivered as I spoke. I listened to Journey and practically knew the room service menu at the Ritz in Paris by heart. I didn't know how to do this. Did people even call heroin *H*? I didn't have a clue. I could con drugs out of just about any doctor in Manhattan, but I couldn't pretend to have street cred. I should have worn my Wu-Tang T-shirt.

"You're looking for H? he said. "That your limo? How much money you got?"

"You know what," I said. "I think maybe I'm in the wrong place." My heart was beating so hard I could hear it.

"Sorry to bother you," I said.

He studied me for a second.

"Grenade," he yelled.

What the fuck?

I took a few steps back and stumbled into a newspaper box that was bolted to the sidewalk behind me. Now, I've never been in the military, but when someone yells *Grenade!* at the top of their lungs, it's probably time to go. I steadied myself and turned to leave.

"Wait there, man," he said. "Here comes Grenade. He's got you."

"That's okay," I said, and starting walking back to the corner.

"Hold up," Grenade called out. I stopped long enough to turn around and see an ox of a man, maybe thirty years old, making his way toward me on a pair of crutches. He wore a white tank top and a pair of low-slung jeans. He was missing his left leg; his pants were folded up and pinned above the knee.

"What did you come here for?" he asked.

I didn't answer and started walking briskly back the way I came.

Grenade's crutches made a distinct sound every time they hit the pavement—like someone walking across a stage with tap shoes.

Clack ... Clack ... Clack.

The frequency of the sound increased.

Clack.Clack.Clack.Clack.

He was running.

So was I.

He was surprisingly agile for an amputee. Much faster than I would have guessed. Or maybe I was far too slow for what the situation demanded. After all, it's not easy to run for your life in a pair of Tod's driving moccasins. Aptly named, if you ask me— they weren't built for running. But then again, neither was I.

"Get your bitch ass out of here," he called.

As I rounded the corner, Billy was leaning on the driver's-side door of the limo smoking a cigarette and listening to one of his books on tape through the open window. Grenade was right behind me.

"Hey," yelled Billy.

Grenade swatted at my leg with his crutches and connected with a loud *clack*. He stopped. I didn't.

I ran about fifty feet to the limo.

"He's gone," Billy said. "Are you all right?"

"I'm fine," I said. I was near tears.

I got in the car and asked him to take me to my hotel.

"What are you looking for?" Billy asked.

"Nothing," I said. "That guy was fucking crazy. Please just get me out of here."

"Listen," said Billy, pulling away from the curb, "if you're looking for something, I may be able to help."

He explained that he had a friend in San Diego who owned a pharmacy and that he was running a little side business for some special clients—including the rock star.

"Can you get me Roxicodone?" I asked.

"No problem," he said. "How many do you want?"

I NEVER DIED

I NEVER DIED.

I thought I might plenty of times. Like a matador stepping into the ring, I was oddly at peace with what could happen and smart enough to know that I might not make it out alive.

But I always did.

I'm probably going to die tonight.

I must have said that to myself—sometimes even out loud—once or twice a week for years.

This might kill me, but fuck it.

I said that, too. A lot. I didn't want to die. Or at least I don't *think* I wanted to die. But I was willing to die. It seemed like an acceptable risk in pursuit of a bigger buzz. A higher high.

I never died.

As a boy, I was terrified of dying. Not in a normal "Hey, I don't want to die" kind of way. Everyone was like that, I guess. No, my fear of death was a little more extreme and made me rather risk averse, to say the least. When I was nine or ten, some of the older neighborhood kids made a ramp out of a milk crate and a rotted two-by-four and tried to jump their dirt bikes—like Evel Knievel—over some younger kids whom they'd dared to lie on the street on the other side of the ramp. This sort of thing gave me anxiety and made me not terribly popular with the BMX set.

"Someone's going to get hurt," I said.

"Okay, Grandma," one of the older kids called back.

"Hey, Danny, your vagina's showing," yelled another.

It didn't help matters when I looked to make sure my fly wasn't down.

But I was right. Someone *did* get hurt that day. The bike didn't even make it up the ramp and instead plowed the milk crate right into the seven-year-old stupid enough to lie there.

"How's my vagina now?" I yelled proudly.

At twelve, I cut my finger while playing with my brother's new Swiss Army knife and was sure I was a goner. We were at our dad's house and I'd sneaked outside with the knife to carve a spear out of a small tree branch. The cut barely deserved a Band-Aid, but my blood-curdling shrieks brought a neighbor rushing over.

"Please tell me I'm not going to die," I pleaded. "Don't let me die."

"I think you'll survive," she said, laughing.

But in the spring of 1974, when I was two years old, I did almost die.

It happened in Miami Beach. I was walking along the edge of the pool at the Carriage House on Collins Avenue when I dropped the small toy I was holding in the water and decided to go in after it.

My family went to Florida for the holidays every year from the time I was a baby. The Carriage House was one of the glamorous beachfront apartment buildings that lined Collins Avenue and served as towering meccas for Baltimore Jews and Long Island Jews and Philadelphia Jews. We all looked the same, with our polo shirts and khaki shorts and Nikes, and we were distinguishable only by our regional accents and the license plates attached to the caravan of Caddies, Lincolns, and Mercedes-Benzes that made their way up and down the avenue.

One afternoon I was playing around the pool and in I went. My brother Jeff, who was four at the time, saw me under the water and ran to tell my mother, who was on a chaise longue about a hundred feet away, playing backgammon with my grandmother. My mom has told me the story dozens of times. How I was sitting calmly at the bottom of the pool, toy in hand. How she screamed for help and a stranger dove in and scooped me up. How my brother had saved my life. How I could have died.

But I didn't.

"YOU COULD HAVE died last night," the doctor said when we first spoke on the phone in early 2003.

"You've been taking *how many* pills a day?" he asked after I just told him that I'd taken over twenty-five Roxicodone the day before. "It's amazing that you're still alive, Dan."

I was scared, but I also felt a sense of pride.

I was uneasy about sharing my secret. I'd been lying to doctors for so long that it felt strange—unnatural, even—telling the truth. Lies had become my truths, and everything else felt fake—especially the truth.

He told me to call him Dr. Ron and that he'd been featured on MTV as one of the pioneers of a rapid detox treatment for heroin and opiate addicts. I found him in the phone book. His ad mentioned the MTV special and had the same red *As Seen on TV* banner that I'd seen on various miracle cleaning products in the grocery store and the Pet Rock my father bought for me when I was a little boy. If I was going to get sober, the least I could do was pick a celebrity recovery doctor. A hint of glamour, I figured, made everything a little less miserable. My dentist, for example, cleaned the teeth of the stars. Signed pictures lined the walls of his Fifth Avenue office—supermodels and actors shaming me with their perfect gleaming grins and healthy gums. Flossers and mid-day brushers, for sure.

"This sounds like a life-or-death situation, Dan," Dr. Ron said. "I'd find a way to come today."

There were no photos of famous patients in Dr. Ron's office. No celebrity endorsements or kind words of thanks scrawled in Sharpie across framed eight-by-tens. I'd taken a car service out to Connecticut, where he had a small office in Stamford. He split his time between there and an office in Manhattan, but if I wanted to see him immediately, he told me, I'd have to leave the city.

He was alone when I got there. A tall, lean man who bore an uncanny resemblance to Martina Navratilova, Dr. Ron took both of my hands into his and guided me into to a chair in the waiting room. He had a small silver hoop in his left ear and wore black onyx Buddhist prayer beads on both wrists. Dr. Ron was built like a distance runner and struck me as the kind of lithe, veiny guy you'd find working at some smelly vitamin and health food shop in the Village.

"You're a doctor, right?" I asked.

"Yes, I am, Dan," he said.

"Like a real doctor?" I said. "An MD? I don't mean to be rude, but I just want to be sure."

"Yes, Dan. I'm a real doctor. You've come to the right place and I think I can help you, because you appear to be trying to help yourself."

He used my name often and spoke with the measured, eerily cheerful tone of a televangelist.

"Based on what you told me over the phone, Dan, it's likely you OD'd last night," he said, sitting down next to me. "To put it even more plainly, you almost died last night."

"For real?" I asked.

"It doesn't get more real than this, Dan," Dr. Ron said. "You're very lucky your girlfriend was with you. She saved your life."

I was being honest with him, but didn't think it was necessary to tell him that my girlfriend was a call girl.

"Wake up! Wake up! You're not breathing."

Chickpea was on her knees on top of the covers shaking me when I opened my eyes. Her hands were gripped onto my left arm and shoulder, her face a few inches away from mine.

"Jesus Christ!" she said. "I've been trying to wake you up for two minutes. Are you okay? You're not breathing."

"I am now," I said, taking a slow, deep breath and propping myself up in bed. I was dizzy. Dizzier than normal, anyway. I was used to being a bit unsteady on my feet when I was high. Sometimes when I woke up in the night to go the bathroom, I would stumble into the bedroom doorjamb or bump the already wobbly wooden nightstand I paid far too much for at the Clignancourt flea market in Paris. I would often pee sitting down to avoid falling or pissing all over the floor.

It took a second for the time illuminated on the cable box's digital display to come into focus. It was after two A.M. A Kevin Costner movie was playing muted on the TV. Chickpea was wearing my NYU hoodie and must have recently taken a hit from the small, colorful glass bowl she kept in her purse, because the bedroom smelled of pot.

"You scared the shit out of me," she said. "Fuck! You weren't breathing. I thought you were dead. I didn't know what to do."

I couldn't help but think that maybe she knew exactly what to do if someone died in bed next to her. Occupational hazard, I figured. One night as we sat in front of the fireplace eating cold pizza she told me that her roommate, Misty, also a call girl with Elegant Affairs, was with a guy at the Four Seasons and she thought he was having a heart attack. He was a famous sportscaster, she told me, and in the middle of rolling around with Misty he went completely white, couldn't catch his breath, and grabbed his chest. Ultimately he was fine, but according to Chickpea, Misty was seconds away from calling 911 and running for the door.

"You were gasping for air," Chickpea said. "Like you were trying to see how long you could hold your breath."

I couldn't have been asleep for more than an hour before she woke me. The pills must have knocked me out. I'd always been something of a night owl, staying up until three or four in the morning watching TV or instructional magic videos or just smoking and sitting on the back deck.

Chickpea got to the apartment after eleven P.M. that night and asked if I minded if she took a shower. Every time she came over, she immediately showered. I never gave any thought to what she was washing away. I didn't care. We had a firm "don't ask, don't tell" policy and it worked for us both. Until that night.

"What's wrong with you?" she asked after it became clear that—like Misty's sportscaster—I wasn't dying.

What's wrong with you?

That question followed me like a vestigial tail.

I'd still hadn't managed to find a suitable answer. What was I going to say? That I had a "what the fuck" moment and took my last four Roxies an hour after my normal evening feeding? That when I opened the door to let her in that night I couldn't see straight? That I was so high my ears were ringing and my face was vibrating?

"I guess I'm just wiped," I said, trying to overpower the sudden need to vomit. "But I'm good."

Nothing says, "What are you talking about? I'm fine!" quite like charging to the bathroom and vomiting. I had become a veteran puker. It usually happened late at night when no one was around, but not always. Like the time I threw up in Times Square. Or when I vomited in the small trash can in my office in the middle of a weekday. I didn't know what to do, so I just lit a scented candle and tried to get some work done.

My assistant came in a few minutes later and busted me. "Dude, did you just vomit in here?" she asked. "It stinks."

"I'm not feeling well," I told her. "It must be something I ate."

I said the same thing to Chickpea and suggested that it might be a rough night and was probably a good idea for her to go home. She didn't argue, of course, which was what made her the ideal "girlfriend" in the first place. We pretended to be a couple when we were together—which was three or four times a week, usually between the hours of midnight and ten A.M. We were both first-rate pretenders and great at ignoring the obvious. I was convinced that if we ran into each other outside of my apartment and either of us was with someone else, we wouldn't have even said hello. Neither of us would have known how to answer the first question anyone would have asked: *How do you guys know each other?* Our relationship was the perfect combination of distance and intimacy. (It would end not long after the night she saved my life. She would move back to Oregon about six weeks later.)

After she left my apartment the night of the OD, I ate. That's what I did when I was worried I'd overdone it and taken too many pills. I ate. What's the old saying? *Starve a fever, feed an overdose.* "Have something to eat," my mother used to say when I complained about not feeling well. I figured that a layer of food—often more bagels—on top of pills might somehow slow them down or dilute them. Addict logic. I did my fair share of middle-of-the-night carbo-loading.

The National Magazine Awards are tomorrow.

That was my first thought—other than taking a second to acknowledge the fact that I was alive—when I woke up the following morning. I immediately started panicking about the awards. The American Society of Magazine Editors was holding its annual awards luncheon the following afternoon at the Waldorf Astoria, and *Details* had three nominations. That meant three potential opportunities to have to go up onstage in front of the publishing industry and speak. That meant hands to shake. That meant small talk. I'd depleted my opiate stash the night before when I took those final four pills. I was out and knew that I couldn't see any of my doctors for at least a week, as it would have been too early to get a refill on any of my prescriptions. That meant withdrawal and that meant trouble.

Dr. Ron wasn't my first choice. I started the day, as I did most days, on a quest for more drugs. I knew the names of the doctors listed in the pain management section of the phone book the way some men knew the starting lineups of the hometown baseball teams from their youth. Albertson. Chatwal. Cole. Orlov. Steinberg. I knew who was in practice with whom and which doctors worked out of hospitals as opposed to their own offices. I knew receptionists and office managers and the proximity of offices to pharmacies. I knew who was inclined to send me for physical therapy or to push for epidural injections. I knew which doctors would write the big prescriptions and that none, sadly, were going to see me on short notice.

And I also knew the panic that was starting to churn inside of me. I couldn't show up at the ASME awards a snotty, sweaty, shivering mess with a clammy handshake and unpredictable bowels—though surely some of the ASME old-timers might.

Panic eventually gave way to fear. I sat cross-legged on my living-room floor flipping through the phone book and trying to think of who I could call to get more drugs. I needed more and I needed them immediately. Maybe there was a way for me to rob Whitney Chemists on University Place, I thought. Like a scene from *Drugstore Cowboy*, I imagined setting fire to the front of the store, where they sold travel umbrellas and oversize fragrant soaps and eccentric reading glasses, and when everyone ran to put out the blaze, I could slip behind the counter and swipe a bottle of pills. It would be only a small fire, not big enough to cause damage to the structure of the building or hurt anyone. Just enough to smoke them out—like bees from a hive. I wouldn't have done it, I don't think, but I considered it often. I had also contemplated renting the apartment directly above University Chemists right across the street from where I lived. At night, when the pharmacy was closed, I figured I could carefully remove the flooring of my apartment and somehow tunnel, *Shawshank* style, into the pharmacy below.

I knew this wasn't normal, of course. Normal people didn't fantasize about breaking into pharmacies or drive to Tijuana to buy a thousand Vicodin. What started as stress about possibly having to miss the National Magazine Awards because I'd be going through withdrawal turned into something far more powerful. I sat chain-smoking on the small Persian rug just in front of the French doors leading to the deck. I was paralyzed with fear.

Did I actually stop breathing last night? Did I really almost die?

I'm still not sure why I did what I did next. I suppose I did what any self-respecting Jewish man does during an emergency. I called my mother. I didn't tell her that I'd stopped breathing while I was sleeping or that a concerned prostitute woke me up—I was sure my mom had a breaking point. But drugs, I figured, she could handle.

"Mom," I said, "I think I've been taking too many painkillers."

Understated, yes, but I didn't want to give her a heart attack.

"It's not that bad," I told her, "but I wanted to let you know I'm going to see a doctor today for help. Don't worry."

Telling a Jewish mother not to worry is like telling a fish not to swim. It's all they know.

"Oh my god. Are you okay?" she asked. "Do you need me to come up?"

"No, Mom," I said. "I'll be okay. I just spoke with a doctor who specializes in this sort of thing and I'm seeing him soon."

"What's his name?" she asked. I was sure this was her way of finding out if he was Jewish, as if that somehow guaranteed better care.

"Don't worry about that, Mom," I said.

And then a question only my mother would ask: "Is this why you haven't been calling me back?"

I'm not sure why I ratted myself out to her. Maybe I wasn't sure I really wanted to stop, and by telling my mother, I was forcing a decision. I was in such a panic. Maybe I needed to hear that everything would be okay. Maybe this was my opportunity to hit the reset button. Perhaps I really was finally ready to stop. I knew one thing for sure: I definitely had a serious drug problem.

Dr. Ron's office wasn't actually Dr. Ron's office. It was a loaner—another doctor's degree framed on the wall and copies of *Newsweek* and *Town & Country* on a small table in the waiting room with someone else's name on the address label.

"I'm only here twice a week for a few hours in the afternoon, Dan," he said. Dr. Ron wore blue surgical scrubs. His bare chest was visible through the shirt's deep V-neck. I'd never been to Stamford and told the driver, one of a network of men in black suits who ferried Condé Nast executives to airports and galas and country houses in black Town Cars, that I needed to see a kidney specialist in Connecticut. Why I felt the need to lie to him or even explain the trip in the first place was beyond me. These guys had seen it all—the affairs and torpedoed careers and god knows what else—and my trip to Stamford would have hardly raised an eyebrow. Still, I lied. I was born with one kidney, I explained, and wanted to make sure it was in "tip-top" shape. I came to learn that good lies always had a shade of truth to them.

When I told Dr. Ron that I had only one kidney, he closed his eyes, exhaled deeply through his nose, and slowly shook his head like a disappointed schoolteacher. "And you've been poisoning your body for how long?" he asked. "With one kidney, Dan. This is the power of addiction. You understand that this is an addiction?"

"I do."

"And you understand, Dan, that you're an addict?"

"Yes," I told Dr. Ron. "I understand."

I couldn't begin to calculate the number of times I'd lied to doctors in order to get what I needed—what my body needed. *Sure, whatever you say*, I'd think to myself, *Just give me the* prescription already and leave me alone. But this time seemed different for some reason. Maybe this kooky guy was right. Maybe I *was* trying to help myself. I mean, I told my mother, for god's sake. Maybe I was done and I didn't want to die after all. Dr. Ron sat quietly and looked at me. His eyes were small but clear and I couldn't find even the hint of stubble on his face.

But did I really want to stop? Or was I there only because I knew he could help ease the dreaded symptoms of withdrawal? I had been pretending to be a "patient" with dozens of doctors and had gotten very convincing. Was I conning Dr. Ron? Was I conning myself?

"I'm scared," I told him as tears welled in my eyes. "I'm tired of feeling this way."

Had the con taken on a life of its own?

"Addicts will do the craziest things," he said. "You know that taking all of those pills might kill you, but you keep going anyway. Like last night, Dan. You kept going. And you overdosed."

I always thought that overdosing meant dying. I didn't know that you could OD and live, but according to Dr. Ron, that's exactly what I'd been doing. All the vomiting and dizziness and gasping for air in the night were symptoms of opiate overdose, he explained. If that was the case, then I was overdosing at least once a week—maybe more.

Doctor Ron told me that the rapid detox had to be scheduled a couple of days in advance, but that he also offered an alternative treatment using buprenorphine injections. Apparently, the buprenorphine tricked the brain into thinking it was an opiate, which it's not, and the body doesn't go through such an aggressive physical detox. I would have to give myself three injections a day—morning, noon, and night—for three days, he explained.

"And I won't go through withdrawal," I asked.

"This treatment will make the physical symptoms of withdrawal much more tolerable," he said. "You won't feel sick. It'll help with the sweating, cramps, and diarrhea."

"I'm in," I told him.

Dr. Ron gave me the first of these shots that afternoon in Stamford and sent me home with a vial of three days' worth of buprenorphine, a handful of alcohol wipes, and eight syringes for the remaining injections. I was to check in with him the following day after the National Magazine Awards to let him know how I was feeling.

I felt an enormous sense of relief. This had been the shortcut I was looking for. I could skip the nightmare of detox and get on with my life. Maybe I was ready to get on with my life.

MY ARMANI SUIT pants were around my knees when I glanced out the window and saw my boss. I actually heard him before I saw him. Patrick's laugh was unmistakable—loud and noticeably higher in pitch than his speaking voice. Not exactly a cackle—less shrill—but easily the least refined feature of an otherwise effortlessly elegant man.

I knew there would be people. And I knew I would know many of them. But it wasn't until I heard the laugh that it dawned on me for the first time that maybe this wasn't a good idea. After all, I was sitting half naked in the back of an idling Town Car on Park Avenue in the middle of the day with the entire publishing industry gathering on the sidewalk just feet away and there was a loaded syringe gripped between my front teeth like a chewed-up Bic pen.

This was definitely a bad idea.

Either way, it was too late. I'd already started. I had no choice but to finish as quickly as I could. Getting caught with my pants down would not have been a good look. I cleaned my thigh with an alcohol wipe and hastily stabbed the needle through my flesh and into the muscle the way the doctor had taught me. I put the cap back on the syringe—being careful not to stick my fingers—and placed it in the inside breast pocket of my suit jacket along with the used wipe. My belt buckle jingled loudly as I haphazardly yanked my pants up with all the grace of a man who's just been caught masturbating in his office cubicle.

I had driven up to the ASME awards with several *Details* editors at around 11:45 A.M. and was planning on giving myself the midday injection in the bathroom at the Waldorf. Lord knows I'd done worse things in there. It wasn't until we were a few blocks away from the hotel that I figured I'd just let my team out of the car and take care of the injection right there, before going in, which in retrospect wasn't the greatest idea.

I was still tucking in my shirt when I caught up to Patrick on the sidewalk.

"Pull yourself together, young man," Patrick said as we walked into the Waldorf.

Every major magazine in the country was represented at the luncheon. *Details* shared a table with some other Condé Nast magazines that had been nominated. I was seated next to Mary Berner, the CEO of Fairchild Publications, a division of Condé. It was a sea of dark suits and day drinkers. I watched as the editors of *Vanity Fair*, the *New Yorker*, and *Sports Illustrated* graciously and eloquently accepted awards. My stomach was turning, but I couldn't tell if it was nerves or my body detoxing.

"That's you," Mary Berner said about an hour into the presentation when they announced that *Details* had won the award for best design. "You better get up there."

Stunned, I stood up and started to make my way to the front of the room. The presenter, who I think was the president of ASME, was still reading the description of *Details* when I got to the bottom of the stairs that led to the stage. This was my moment. I had arrived. "Accepting the award is David Peres, editor in chief of *Details*."

Really? I thought. *Did she just call me David?*

Still, up I went, Dr. Ron's spent syringe in my pocket, to accept the award. Si Newhouse was standing there at my table when I returned, a huge grin on his face and his hand outstretched. I'd never seen him in a suit before.

"Well done, Dan," he said. "Look what you've done. Unbelievable."

If he only knew.

WITH THE HELP of Dr. Ron's injections, I remained sober . . . for four days. I filled a prescription for several hundred Roxicodone early the following week.

WARNINGS AND CONSEQUENCES

I IGNORED THE WARNINGS.

There were a lot of warnings and I ignored them all. I was sure that they weren't there for me. I was a seasoned user. The warnings were there to caution newcomers, weekend warriors, and occasional dabblers. Not me. So I ignored them.

The stickers—like colorful fortune-cookie fortunes—were stuck to the side of the prescription bottle. *Do not drink alcoholic beverages when taking this medication. May cause nausea. Do not operate dangerous machinery.* Important reminders, for sure, but I ignored them all.

CAUTION: MAY CAUSE DROWSINESS.

The cigarette burns in my sofa cushions should have been a sign. Or the ones on my sheets. Or the burns just below the knuckles between the index and middle fingers of my right hand.

I was nodding out and I was smoking way too much. Not an ideal combination.

But I had no idea this was happening. Maybe I'd been careless or distracted, I figured. Or maybe I was just too high to even care.

I'd simply flip the sofa cushion and buy new sheets. Addict problem solving at its finest.

I'd never been a great sleeper. When we were growing up, my brother, Jeff, who was two and a half years older than I was, went to bed well before I did. I'd stay up late—sometimes until midnight—practicing magic tricks and watching Johnny Carson, also a magician, on the small television in my room. I'd pretend to be a guest on his show and wow him with my cunning sleight of hand and witty banter. My mom was a night owl, too, and would pop in my room or call down to me in the basement to tell me to go to bed.

"It's time," she'd say.

But it was never time. I couldn't fall asleep. So I went on playing. Nights were perfect for me—forced solitude. No homework or dinner-table conversation or quick trips to the grocery store with my mom. Nights were for me.

I never grew out of it.

When I was living in Paris, I would often ride my bike along the quiet Left Bank streets well after midnight. It was as if I never got over the jet lag from the flight over. The lights on the Eiffel Tower went out at one A.M. I know this because I watched it happen many times, sitting on my blue Peugeot mountain bike in the Champs de Mars by the base of the iron landmark.

Nights were for daydreaming. Sometimes I was a famous magician. Other times a successful writer. I was always well known in these little fantasies—a sought-after celebrity seeking privacy and living along the Quai d'Orsay or in one of those great brownstones on 10th Street between Fifth and Sixth.

Nights were also for drugs. The best highs were the ones when everyone else was sleeping and there was no one around to ask me why I wasn't.

Initially, the pills knocked me out. When they were first given to me after my back surgery and I was taking them as prescribed, they did what they were designed to do—dull the pain and help me get some rest. This didn't last long. By the time I was into my first year as editor in chief of *Details*, with the pain long gone, I'd become convinced that they gave me energy—that I needed them to get through the day.

I'll be fine once I get some Vicodin in me, I thought to myself on many mornings. *This will wake me up.*

Mornings were rough, and I often slept till 9:30 or 10:00 A.M., around the same time the *Details* staff was getting to the office. I might not have fallen asleep easily, but when I slept, I slept hard.

On September 11, 2001, I was still sleeping when my girlfriend, Caroline, called and woke me at ten that morning. She was crying.

"Are you okay?" she asked. "Where are you?"

"I'm about to walk to the subway," I said, lying. "I've been on a conference call for the last hour."

Conference calls were my go-to excuse for still being home at that hour. There were lots of them. I'd occasionally mix it up and say I was at a breakfast meeting with a writer or was sitting in a coffee shop reading through articles for an upcoming issue, but conference calls were my default.

"You haven't seen the news?" Caroline asked, exasperated. "Or heard the sirens?"

Despite living on 11th Street at the time and being just a few miles from Ground Zero, I hadn't heard a thing. I'm surprised I even heard the phone ring when she called.

"Who could you be talking to right now?" she asked.

She had a point. The whole world knew what was going on. I was pretty sure she didn't buy it.

Pills consumed my life. Getting them. Taking them. Running out of them. This was my routine. Anything else—everything else—didn't matter. Family, friends, and work were barely on my radar—faded blips in the distance. My priority was drugs. Napping was a close second. Needless to say, this made scheduling appointments with me challenging. Some people at the magazine had taken to calling my assistant "the Rescheduler."

I was living in a floor-through of the same brownstone on 11th Street that had been my first home in New York after returning from Paris. I'd wanted to be close to NYU, where I went to school, and this apartment was just steps from University Place. The brownstone, with purple wisteria climbing its brick front, was separated into four units. Mine was on the third floor. Adam Horovitz from the Beastie Boys had lived there before me (a short-term rental while he renovated his own house), and he was there to show me around when I first went to take a look. "It's a great place," he told me, "but most of the apartment doesn't get much light." Just what I was looking for.

Horovitz obviously wasn't referring to the bedroom, which as fate would have it faced south onto 11th Street and was flooded with direct sunlight that made napping a challenge. Shades were already attached to the room's two gigantic windows, but I installed drapes for good measure. Natural light was the enemy. I was shamed by the sun. With the shades drawn and the drapes closed, this room became my refuge during the day. When I wasn't at the office, where I was spending only four or five hours on a good day, I was camped out on my bed. I ate there, watched TV there, talked to the office there, and napped there. When I wasn't on the bed, I was straightening it. Every time I would climb off, I would take a minute to smooth out the comforter and prop up the pillows. Making the bed helped me forget that I had just been asleep in the middle of the day, like shaking an Etch A Sketch clean.

On the opposite end of the apartment was a sizable deck facing the backs of the buildings on 12th Street. It overlooked the outdoor seating for a little Mexican restaurant on University where Christmas lights dangled year-round from a wooden trellis surrounding about eight tables. I spent many nights sitting quietly at a small table on my deck, numbed by Vicodin, smoking Marlboro Mediums as the City That Never Sleeps slept around me.

I even napped at the office on occasion.

"I'm going to be reading some copy in here," I'd tell the Rescheduler before closing my office door. "Please keep people away for about a half hour."

And then I'd lie down on the sofa—shoes on—and crash.

Naps were one thing, but I didn't realize I was actually nodding out until the job interview.

Some of the other editors and I had been talking about trying to hire Jason for some time. He was a rising star at *New York* magazine, as both a writer and an editor, and I'd been following his work there for the better part of a year. Our features editor had recently decamped to a competing magazine and we decided to go after Jason, who only a month earlier had been passed over for a bigger role at *New York*.

"I think we can get him," Andrew said. "I met him for a drink last night and he's definitely open to the possibility."

The executive editor of *Details*, Andrew was a peerless networker and as shrewd and persuasive a schmoozer as there was. He, along with the team that we had assembled, made it possible for the magazine to get out every month. I may have been loaded on Vicodin half the time, but I was brimming with story ideas and was able to hand them off to Andrew and the rest of the team to execute, which they did brilliantly. Jason would have made a great addition to the magazine's masthead, so the Rescheduler scheduled a time for us to meet.

"Please don't cancel on him," said Andrew. "I need you to close the deal."

By the time I met Jason in 2003, I was taking pills in order to function. I couldn't get out of bed without them. The highs weren't as high as they'd once been, but without the pills, I was a mess and in a constant state of withdrawal. They were a part of my daily routine—as essential as food and water. More so, even.

I could barely keep my eyes open when Jason and I sat down to talk at the wooden conference table in my office. He congratulated me on winning the National Magazine Award on the bookshelf behind me. I held a copy of his résumé as we spoke. I felt my eyes closing.

"Please forgive me," I said. "I have a migraine coming on and need to close my eyes for a bit while we talk. Weird, I know, but it helps."

The lies came quickly and often. Some were better than others.

"No problem," he said.

"Have you seen our current issue?" I asked, eyes closed. "What do you think about the mix of features?"

"I think you guys have some good stuff in there," I remember Jason saying from the other side of the table. "But I think you might benefit from more . . ."

I was out—like a drug-addled narcoleptic, sitting upright, résumé in hand. My head tipped forward and then quickly bounced back as if on a spring, jolting me awake. I opened my eyes and pretended to study the résumé. Jason was still talking.

"Go on," I said as I got up from the table and asked my assistant to bring me a Diet Coke.

I drank at least five or six Diet Cokes a day. There was a mini-fridge full of them under her desk. They were my magic elixir, chugged from a large red Solo cup, like I was playing quarters at a fraternity party.

The conversation with Jason continued for another twenty-five minutes. I was awake for the rest of the interview, most of it spent wondering whether he saw me nod out. We offered him the job of features director the following day.

He declined.

Now I knew. I was nodding out. And while it should have scared me, it didn't. It became just another in a series of confounding behaviors that I was sure could be covered up with a quality lie. Going forward, whenever I felt tired in the middle of the day, I blamed it on the fact that I had only one kidney and that my body was producing too many red blood cells.

"My blood is thicker than normal," I explained. "It zaps me of my energy. I'm dealing with it. I've been going to tons of doctor appointments, which is why I haven't been around so much lately."

One lie to solve two problems—the nodding out and my constant absences from the office. I was particularly proud of this one.

But I knew it needed to stop. That *I* needed to stop. I'd seen Dr. Ron, the addiction specialist, three times in as many months, but every time—after a few days of injecting buprenorpine into my thighs and swearing off painkillers—I was right back at it.

"These shots aren't the answer," Dr. Ron told me. "They don't cure addiction. They're just here to help you manage the symptoms of withdrawal. You need to go to meetings. You need more help than I alone can give you."

I didn't realize how true that was until the summer of 2003, when I was in Milan for fashion week. I never liked Milan. I referred to it as the Trenton of Italy—industrial and bleak. There were some beautiful areas, of course, like the historic Brera district in the heart of the city, home to the Duomo and La Scala and the Four Seasons Hotel. Most of the city, though, was gray and depressing and reminded me of Soviet Bloc housing. I dreaded going.

There were, however, two upsides—pasta and pills. Doctors in Milan, unlike those in Paris, could prescribe the same powerful opiates I was getting in America.

I'd been going to Milan at least four times a year since taking over as editor of *Details*. In addition to the men's fashion shows that I attended for a week every January and June, I went several times a year for meetings—one-on-ones with designers and fashion executives. Most of the revenue that the magazine made came from luxury fashion advertising—brands like Giorgio Armani, Versace, and Dolce & Gabbana—making Milan a frequent destination.

Nothing eases the burden of being in a city you hate like staying in the Four Seasons Hotel. A converted fifteenth-century convent, the Four Seasons in Milan is one of the chicest hotels in the world. Tucked away on the relatively quiet Via Gesù and just a few doors down from the sprawling, art-filled home where Gianni Versace used to live, the Four Seasons was the best part of every trip to Milan.

"Ciao, Signore Peres," the doorman would say as I stepped out of the car. I loved this in any language.

They always gave me the same room, 262, which was the size of a large New York City studio apartment and had a huge marble bathroom, stocked with fragrant Bvlgari soaps and shampoos that I used to stuff into my Dopp kit and take with me. It didn't matter where I was, I smelled like I'd showered at the Four Seasons in Milan.

I once stayed in room 262 for most of fashion week, because I didn't have enough Vicodin to get me through the week and I got sick. I spent four days in a plush terry cloth robe sipping broth from room service and having housekeeping clean the room around me.

This was before I knew I could get opiates there, which I did on two occasions. The first time, I asked the front desk to send an English-speaking doctor to the room. Within thirty minutes, a friendly bearded man with round tortoiseshell glasses showed up. I performed my standard back pain routine and he wrote me a large prescription. Piece of cake.

The second time, about a year and a half later, was more challenging. I was taking sixty pills a day by this point—fifteen every four hours—but had run out the previous night. Early the following morning, I called down to the front desk to ask if they could arrange for a doctor to see me. Thirty minutes later, the same bearded man with round tortoiseshell glasses was at my door. I hadn't considered that this might be a possibility. I pretended that we'd never met.

"I remember you," he said after I put on quite a show of hobbling across the room to illustrate how bad my back was. "I've seen you before, yes?"

"I think you may be right," I said. "What are the odds? This has happened only one other time since I had my back surgeries. Maybe I should stop coming to Milan?"

He wasn't amused, but wrote me a prescription anyway, though for far fewer pills than he had the last time.

"The farmacia will give you thirty tablets," he said, handing me the prescription. "Next time be sure to travel with your medication. I won't be giving you any more drugs."

I filled the prescription at the pharmacy around the corner from the hotel and raced back to my room to take the pills and get ready for another day of back-to-back fashion shows. I could feel the drugs kicking in while I was in the shower—the warm tingling sensation that I'd come to need to function.

With a few minutes to spare, I sat on the edge of the king-size bed wearing the white robe that was hanging in the bathroom, lit a cigarette, and tuned the television to CNN. The next thing I knew, I felt like I was slipping. Startled, I jolted upright. I had nodded out. The cigarette I'd been holding was next to me on the bed; a hole the size of a half-dollar was still smoldering at the edges in the top sheet. I quickly patted it out with the palm of my right hand before dousing it with what was left in the green glass bottle of San Pellegrino on the nightstand.

I put on a navy blue suit and left for the Dolce & Gabbana show.

DONNA

WHAT'S WRONG WITH YOU?

By 2004, the doctors were asking. Their receptionists were asking. The pharmacists at the small mom-and-pop pharmacies were asking.

Even if they weren't saying the words, I could see it in their eyes when I came to the office for a prescription refill weeks before I was scheduled to.

I could feel it in the way they crossed their arms when I explained that I'd lost the pill bottle on a recent trip here or there. And I could tell they were talking about me when they left the exam room to get my file.

What had begun in 2000 as a well-rehearsed and polished performance for every doctor I saw was becoming harder to consistently pull off. After a few years, I'd started phoning it in and the cracks were definitely beginning to show.

But this wasn't always the case. In the beginning, the con was flawless.

The act would start well before I got to the door of the doctor's office, sometimes even when I was still a block or two away. What if the receptionist or nurse was out getting a coffee and saw me walking normally? I wasn't about to take the risk. No, I got into character the moment I stepped out of the taxi or climbed the stairs from the subway. Like a method actor, I would limp down the street, sometimes dragging my right foot behind me like a ball and chain. I moved slowly and deliberately, stopping often to rest my leg and rub the small of my back, my face scrunched in pain. It was the most committed I'd ever been to anything.

By the time I limped into the doctor's office, I was out of breath, awkwardly lowering myself into the waiting-room chair like an expectant mother.

I had been seeing three different pain management specialists a month, supplemented by new doctors—often neurologists— when necessary. These were the one-offs—the quick fixes for when I was in a jam—who wrote small prescriptions that I'd use to tide me over. The pain doctors were my bread and butter. They were more comfortable prescribing large amounts in higher doses. Their practices were made up of people in chronic pain—cancer patients and accident victims. I'd often have to step around their canes and walkers as I made my way back to see the doctor. They were in agony, misery seared on their faces. I used them as inspiration to hone my performance.

Once every six months or so, one of the doctors would ask me to get an MRI so they could see what was going on with my spine. I happily obliged. Thanks to that disastrous cartwheel attempt years earlier, not to mention the scar tissue from my two surgeries, these MRIs always showed a messed-up spine and bulging discs—an unfakable prop that made the act all the more believable. And they all bought it. I always showed up clean-shaven and often wearing a suit, even on the days—and there were a lot of them— when I was going through withdrawal, my skin crawling, my heart racing, and my body aching for a fix. Those were the Oscar-worthy performances. I had to dig deep on those days, but in the end, it worked. I didn't look like an addict. This was before opiate addiction was a national crisis. Before the CNN specials and the presidential commissions. This was before nice Jewish boys from towns like Pikesville who went to summer camp and did magic tricks looked like addicts.

It always worked. I got all the pills I needed. Until I started to need more. I was feeding an addiction that had become insatiable. My tolerance had grown so high that the monthly prescriptions I was getting from the three different doctors combined—over eight hundred pills—barely lasted two weeks.

The con got more elaborate.

"I'm going on a two-week tour of Italian luxury goods factories for work," I told Donna. "And then I'm taking a well-deserved vacation for a couple of weeks with my new girlfriend. We're going to visit her family in Australia. It's getting serious."

Donna was Dr. Stanley Fine's sister and office manager. She ran the show. Nothing happened in that office without Donna knowing about it. She was in her early sixties and wore a white lab coat over her clothes. She was the widowed mother of two sons. One was a dermatologist with a new practice in Edison, New Jersey, and the other was a freelance journalist who'd written an unproduced play about John Wilkes Booth.

"Maybe my son should be writing for your magazine," she'd say.

"Of course," I always replied. "Please put him in touch. We're always looking for dermatologists who can write."

"Oy. If you were my son, I'd smack your face," she'd say.

This was our shtick. I saw Donna at least once a month for three years and it was the same thing every time. I knew how to con a Jewish mom. I'd been conning my own for years.

Just to play it safe, I had my assistant call the Condé Nast travel

agency and have them put together an itinerary showing flights
from New York to Milan and then, two weeks later, from Milan
to Sydney. A trip I would never take. I didn't even stop to consider
what my assistant might be thinking; I didn't care. I had been
conning her, too, of course, but with far less dedication. Plus, I
was starting to nod out in the office. Odds were that she knew I
was a mess. That I could deal with, but for Donna, I needed to put
on a good show.

"I know I'm a week early for my prescription," I said, handing
her the itinerary, "but this trip is happening, and I don't want to
be without my medication while I'm away."

Medication. I never really considered it medication. Maybe when
it was first prescribed to me around the time of my surgery, but it
hadn't been medicine in years. They were simply my pills. My fuel.
I could count the hours of the day by how many pills I had left in
my pocket, like beads on an abacus. They were so many things to
me, those pills—fuel, an escape, and eventually a necessity—but
medication was not one of them.

"Let me see if I can grab Stanley," Donna said. "Wait here."

Donna had Dr. Fine write me a prescription and asked to keep
the itinerary for my file. I hobbled back out onto the sidewalk
and limped my way to the subway.

A few months later, I called Donna on her direct line and asked
if I could come in to see the doctor in between my normal monthly
appointments.

"Didn't we just see you a few weeks ago?" she asked.

"Yeah, I know. I have another big trip planned. We're launching
an English version of the magazine and I'm going to be in London
for three weeks hiring a staff," I said, lying. "I'm dreading it."

As if somehow dread made the lie more convincing. The rate
at which I was running out of pills impacted the con as much as it

did my ability to function. Taking massive amounts of opiates has its share of powerful side effects, and lying should be at the top of the list.

"Sure, Dan," Donna said after a long pause. "Come on in."

That afternoon I got my pain face on and shuffled into Dr. Fine's office. Donna was perched behind the counter, where she always was, talking on the phone. She didn't smile at me the way she normally did. She just waved me over and held up her finger, signaling she'd just be a minute.

She eventually brought me into the doctor's office—a small, cluttered room with a large wooden desk barely visible under a blanket of papers and files. Stacks of drug samples in colorful boxes sat on top of a black metal filing cabinet. Nothing worth stealing—I always checked. I also scanned the desk for a prescription pad, but no luck. I'd never stolen one, but I'd fantasized about it, to the point that it was totally normal for me to quickly go through drawers when I was left alone in an exam room—cautiously listening for footsteps on the other side of the closed door.

While I'd never written a prescription before, I did pretend to be a doctor once and called in a prescription to a pharmacy, back when Vicodin could be called in over the phone. I kept an unfilled prescription that a neurologist, Dr. Kornbluth, once wrote for me for a muscle relaxer. This would happen in the early days. Doctors would try to give me drugs I had no use for until I eventually just started asking for exactly what I wanted. One night shortly after 9/11, when I was a sweaty, dope-sick mess and contemplating yet another trip to the emergency room, I fished out the unused script. I had no idea what I was doing or if it would work, but I'd been in the room once when a doctor called in a prescription for me. The key, I learned, was to have a DEA number—a unique series of nine letters and numbers assigned to doctors by the Drug Enforcement

Administration allowing them to prescribe controlled substances. It was ten P.M. and I called the twenty-four-hour pharmacy at 14th Street and Fourth Avenue and impersonated Dr. Kornbluth.

"Patient's name?" the pharmacist asked.

Oh, right. I need to give a name. I hadn't thought this through.

"Joseph Silver," I said, giving my grandfather's name after a moment of panic.

I read Kornbluth's DEA number off the prescription and asked for thirty Vicodin—one to two every four to six hours as needed for pain—and held my breath.

"Patient's birthdate?" the pharmacist asked. I told him my grandfather's birthday.

"Okay. All set," the pharmacist said. "Have a good night, Doctor."

Terrified I might get arrested, I nervously walked into the pharmacy thirty minutes later, wearing a blue Nike baseball cap pulled down low, the brim nearly covering my eyes, like I was casing the joint, and picked up my dead grandfather's prescription.

Donna didn't mention anything about her son's writing for the magazine this time. Instead, she sat down behind Dr. Fine's desk and asked if I was okay, a look of genuine concern on her face.

"We can't give you the prescription, Dan," she said. "You've been coming in too often. Dr. Fine and I are worried about you."

This was serious. Donna had always referred to him as Stanley when she spoke to me. It was only a matter of time until this happened. I'd become desperate and it was showing.

"Why?" I asked.

"Dan, you know we adore you," she said, "but we think that maybe you have a problem. Are you taking the medication as prescribed?"

"Of course I am," I said with a touch of indignation. "Why would you ask that? I can't control how much traveling I have to do for my job, Donna. I wish I could."

"This just doesn't seem normal," she said.

There was that word again—*normal*—stuck to me like some junkie scarlet letter. She knew. The blood drained from my face. I wanted so badly to stop the charade. It was exhausting—all of the scheming and lying. I'd been trying since my first visit to Dr. Ron, and here was my chance to come clean with Donna. I genuinely liked her. I could cry with her, tell her everything. She was a Jewish mom. She'd hug me and tell me everything would be okay. I believed it when she said that she and Stanley adored me. Maybe they could help? Maybe this was the answer? But the fear of not having the pills, of going through the withdrawal, of living life without, overpowered any instinct I had to tell the truth. I needed drugs, not truth.

Cornered, I clung to my lie and lashed out. "What are you suggesting?" I demanded.

"I think you're addicted to the medication and that you're abusing it, Dan," she said matter-of-factly. "It happens all the time. It's okay."

"Nothing about this is okay," I said. "And I resent the accusation."

"Let me get Dr. Fine and the three of us can discuss this," Donna said. "I'm not trying to upset you, but we feel like you need some help."

"Help," I said. "The only help I need is for my back. Look at me, I can't even stand up straight."

I exhaled deeply, put my hands on my thighs, and slowly rocked back and forth in the chair. The con was over, but I wouldn't let go. Not yet. Maybe I could turn it around.

I dug in. "Listen, I know all about addiction," I said. "The magazine has published a bunch of stories about it over the years. I'm terrified of it. I'm the last guy who would ever abuse medication like this."

"Okay," she said. "But we can no longer have you as a patient here. Dr. Fine will recommend another doctor for you."

"Wait. Please don't do this," I said, like some poor soul refusing to accept that his girlfriend was dumping him.

"I'm sorry," she said. "This is our decision."

"Fine," I said. "You couldn't be more wrong, but fine."

I stood up slowly, using the arms of the office chair to push myself up. My cover may have been blown, but I stayed in character.

"I'll leave," I said as Donna stood from behind the desk. I could tell that this was hard for her.

I limped down the hall.

"Please don't leave," Donna said. "Let us help you."

"First do no harm," I said, stopping and turning to talk to her. "Isn't that what doctors say? Isn't that part of the Hippocratic Oath?"

I'm not sure where that came from, but I was ad-libbing at this point. This was unfamiliar territory, and I felt like I'd just been punched in the gut. Part of it was that I needed the pills, of course, but I also didn't want Donna to think poorly of me.

"Well, guess what?" I said. "You are doing a lot of harm right now."

"Come on, Dan. Why won't you sit down with the doctor and discuss this?" she said as I hobbled out the door. "What's wrong with you?"

ROCK STAR REDUX

"ROCK STARS DON'T WEAR SHORTS," I tell the rock star.

"What the fuck are you talking about? Angus Young wears shorts all the time," he says, a Marlboro bobbing up and down in his mouth like a conductor's baton.

"Not tennis shorts," I say.

We're standing on the sandstone back deck of his modern Beverly Hills estate, which—in addition to an infinity pool and the small guesthouse, where I slept for a few hours after we called it quits at four A.M.—has a tennis court.

Even after he tells me he plays once a week, it's impossible for me to picture the man I just spent the night chain-smoking cigarettes and snorting lines of oxy with lunging for a forehand.

The L-shaped house is framed by concrete and wood with floor-to-ceiling glass walls. It is surprisingly tasteful, particularly given the fact that the rock star had a fanny pack with him the first time we met. People with fanny packs don't live in houses like this. Architects do. Or power agents. The property is walled in by perfectly maintained eight-foot-tall hedges, which seem to be standard issue for the neighborhood.

I didn't notice the tennis court the night before when I stumbled down to the guesthouse—so high and exhausted that I wasn't sure I could make the twenty-yard walk without tipping over or, worse, ending up in the pool. I was a solitary drug user and I wasn't used to snorting oxy. I was higher than I was used to being, which is saying a lot.

For as uncontrollable as my drug use had become, there was a fair amount of control involved. I knew exactly how many pills I needed to get buzzed: fifteen extra-strength Vicodin; seven 15-milligram Roxicodone; twenty-one 5-milligram Roxicodone. Even though I'd been taking more at times, it was simple math, more or less, and snorting them messed with the equation. How many pills are ground up in this pile? Is one line equivalent to one pill? How much has the rock star snorted as opposed to what I was inhaling? It was impossible to know. Drug addiction isn't an exact science, but I tried to operate with the precision of a chemist. Getting high with the rock star was like flying blind.

I hadn't planned on spending the night. Billy drove me to the rock star's house at 10:30 P.M. after a business dinner in West Hollywood. The plan was to hang out with the rock star for a bit and divvy up the large bottle of 80-milligram OxyContin that Billy brought us from San Diego. Then I was going back to L'Ermitage hotel, where I sometimes stayed when I was in Los Angeles. It didn't work out that way. Plans seldom do with junkies.

I'd been spending a lot of time in LA. Aside from the usual reasons for me to fly out there—meetings with publicists, cover shoots, the occasional event the magazine was hosting in honor of a celebrity—my new girlfriend, Sarah, lived there. She was a beautiful and talented Australian-born actress whom I'd met a few months earlier at a mutual friend's beach house in Malibu. She was, as usual, way out of my league.

The first time I saw Sarah felt like a scene out of an eighties romantic comedy:

EXTERIOR—DECK OF SEVENTIES-ERA MALIBU BEACH HOUSE—DAY

Fade In

It's a perfect Southern California day. Boy in shorts and T-shirt walks out onto the deck. His legs are as white as the sand below. Boy notices breathtaking girl in a bikini reading a script. He's immediately tongue-tied. Girl politely says hello.

    SARAH

Hello. Nice to meet you. I'm Sarah.

Boy tries to make small talk, awkwardly commenting on the color of the ocean.

    DAN

Hi. I'm Dan. Wow, look how blue the ocean is. Amazing.

Girl smiles at boy, then looks out at the ocean just beyond the deck, politely confirming that it is in fact blue.

    SARAH

Yes, it is.

Boy stands around for a few seconds, hands in pockets. Unimpressed by his silence, girl takes a sip from her Evian bottle and goes back to her reading. Boy exits, nervous and smitten.

    Fade Out

It took me ten minutes to get up the courage to go back outside and speak with her. Normally I could talk to anyone, but there was something about this woman that made me nervous. It was the first time in a long time that I wanted to flirt, and I was rusty.

I eventually sat down next to her and started a conversation. She was funny and smart and couldn't have been the least bit romantically interested in me. I tried to flirt, but she was having none of it. She did, however, agree to give me her email address before she left later that afternoon.

From that moment on, I saw Sarah everywhere. Literally. On my flight back to New York the following day, I was flipping through an issue of one of the celebrity weeklies—*People* or *Us*—and there was a photo of her shimmering on a red carpet. In a taxi the very next day, I drove past a Gap ad on a billboard and there she was—fourteen feet tall, her skin golden brown, gazing out over the city.

In the chaotic, unpredictable world I'd created for myself, Sarah had suddenly—and inexplicably—emerged as a presence. I began emailing her and we quickly became friends. We saw each other a few times over the next few months, either when she was in New York or I was back in LA. Being with her, even as friends, somehow calmed me. I eventually wore her down and we starting dating. I would fly out to see her as often as I could.

Trips to LA also meant seeing Billy. Ever since the night he had driven me to the sketchy heart of Hollywood on my quest for heroin, I called Billy when I was in town. It wasn't that I felt beholden to throw business his way as a thank-you for saving me from an uncertain fate at Grenade's hands. No. My rationale was far less altruistic than that. Billy could get pills. Lots of them.

And he never once asked, "What's wrong with you?"

Billy is listening to Michael Connelly's *City of Bones* when I climb into the back seat of his black Town Car outside the American terminal at LAX. Detective Harry Bosch is investigating the case of a young boy who'd gone missing twenty years earlier. He hands me a small bottle of water from the red and white Playmate cooler on the passenger seat and ejects the audiobook. "Come Sail Away" by Styx plays on the radio as we make our way toward the 405.

"Dennis DeYoung is a good guy," Billy says. "A real sweetheart. I've had him in my car a couple of times. Some of these musicians are real pricks, you know. But Dennis is a kind soul."

There are as many nice-guy celebrity stories in LA as there are producers, and Billy is loaded with them.

"But you also get the assholes," he says. "The ones who keep you waiting all night, not telling me when or if they might be coming out. I mean, how hard is it to let me know it's okay for me to run and grab a slice of pizza or take a piss, for Christ's sake? I keep an empty one-gallon water jug in the trunk in case of emergencies. And I've had to use it plenty of times."

"Man, that sucks," I said. I was sympathetic—but couldn't help but think about my Louis Vuitton duffel in the trunk. "Listen, take it easy on these turns," I said as we rolled into Beverly Hills.

"You got it," said Billy, barely missing a beat before jumping right back into his detailed account of celebrity client behavior. "I'm telling you man, you wouldn't believe some of the shit that's gone on in the back seat of this car. Man, people have been fully naked back there—you don't want to know."

"No shit, I don't want to know," I said, scanning the back seat in disgust. "I'm sitting back here. I don't want to hear this."

But it was true. Car service drivers see and hear everything. Condé Nast was famous for having a fleet of black Town Cars and SUVs on hand for its senior management. They lined the street in front of the company's New York headquarters like an idling funeral procession. There was even a guy, Red, whose only job, as far as I could tell, was to wait outside the building and direct us to whichever car was ours when we came through the revolving door, like an air traffic controller for aimless executives.

These drivers often knew who was about to be fired or promoted well before it was public knowledge. They knew who was sleeping with whom and which executive was getting a divorce and who was having long, drunken lunches at the Four Seasons.

"I hear [publishing exec] is on the way out," one of the Condé drivers told me once. "They can't stand him. Plus, he's been screwing his assistant for over year. They're trying to avoid a lawsuit."

I'm sure that the guys who drove me, whether in New York or when I was traveling for business, knew more about what was going on with me than just about anyone else. Doctor visits, pharmacy runs, and if they were paying attention—and they always were—they would have seen me shovel hundreds of pills into my mouth over the years. It was only a matter of time until I found a driver who could supply them.

I'd seen Billy close to a dozen times since we'd met a year earlier. He lived in San Diego and would drive up with pills for his "special clients" from his friend's pharmacy once a week. Billy had been supplying the rock star with oxy for a few years, making him—and now me—one of only a small handful of people who knew that the rock star was still using. The rock star's struggles with alcoholism and addiction had been well documented by the tabloids.

The first two times I saw Billy, he didn't drive me. It was just a good old-fashioned drug deal. We met in the parking lot of Factor's Famous Deli on Pico. Like any good Jewish boy, I was able to score drugs and a corned beef on rye at the same time. The third time I called him, Billy offered to get me at the airport. "It'll just be easier," he said. "It'll help me justify the trip up to LA." He also asked if I would mind his telling the rock star that he was getting me pills. Billy could get only large quantities. "It's not worth it for my friend at the pharmacy if it's a small amount," he said, and suggested that the rock star and I might want to share the pills . . .

and the cost. At first I found this a little odd. If I could afford the drugs—$1,500 for a bottle of four hundred pills—then surely the rock star could. But I agreed.

First, we had to find a compromise. The rock star preferred 80-milligram OxyContin, while I favored 15-milligram Roxicodone.

"Let's each get what we like," I told the rock star after Billy put us in touch. "It'll give this pharmacy guy twice as much business."

"Let's just split a bottle for now," he said. "Maybe we can alternate—Roxys this time. Oxys the next. It'll make it easier for me."

Also odd, but I said yes.

This went on for the better part of a year. Occasionally, Billy would take me from the airport straight to the rock star's house, where we'd split up the pills and smoke a couple of cigarettes. Still eager to launch a fashion line, the rock star would show me some of his designs and ask for feedback. It was bad LA fashion—studded leather belts and wrist cuffs and some Ed Hardy–inspired T-shirts and snapback hats haphazardly covered with rhinestones.

"Rock and roll, right?" he'd say proudly.

"Totally," I'd say. "Very LA."

BILLY WAS STILL talking about his famous passengers when we pulled up to L'Ermitage. The buzz from the eight Roxicodone I'd taken on the flight over was starting to fade, not that it had been especially satisfying. Plane highs were usually the best, especially in first class. A comfortable reclining chair with a footrest. Cabin lights dimmed. A selection of movies. And the freedom to nod out without being self-conscious. Everybody dozed off on planes. Everybody except addiction specialist to the stars Dr. Drew Pinsky, who, as fate would have it, was seated directly beside me on this flight. Talk about a buzzkill. It was like sitting next to a narc.

He definitely knows I'm high, I thought, avoiding eye contact with him every time I climbed over his legs on my way to the bathroom. *Don't let him see your pupils.*

I didn't even know if opiates did anything to your pupils or why Dr. Drew would even care. It's not like he was going to stage an intervention at 30,000 feet. Still, I wasn't taking any risks.

"Always tons of celebrities at L'Ermitage," Billy said as he pulled up to the curb.

He was right. I had been staying at L'Ermitage since I got the *Details* job, and the crowd in the lobby bar rarely disappointed. As was often the case, the bars at swanky Beverly Hills hotels were as star-studded as back lots. Well-known actors taking meetings with agents and producers while sipping cocktails and snacking on wasabi peas.

"Taking meetings." That's what they called it. It was never just "having a drink" or "grabbing lunch." They were "taking meetings." LA cracked me up.

Billy was going to wait for me while I got settled in my room and showered before taking me to my dinner with the head of marketing for an independent production company and then to the rock star's house, where I ultimately ended up spending the night.

"I'll be about an hour," I told him. "Feel free to grab a slice, and for the love of God, if you have to pee, come in and use the bathroom in the lobby."

The minimalist rooms at L'Ermitage were large, bright, and monotone. The blond wood furniture matched the tan rug and drapes. I preferred to face the back of the hotel, to avoid any noise from the street. Being on New York time in Los Angeles, where it was three hours earlier, meant I was able to sleep later than usual. Mornings are the enemy of the addict.

Sarah was out of town working on a television show in Van-
couver. Lately I'd been staying with her at her house perched high
in the Hollywood Hills whenever I was in LA. And while I missed
her, I was happy to be alone in a hotel room, free to use. Sarah—
like my mother and Adam—thought I was sober. I'd told them
that I hadn't taken a painkiller since the first time I saw Dr. Ron.
They were all incredibly proud of me, which stung a bit, but I
think, deep down, they all knew the truth—maybe not every day
or even every month, but I figured that my erratic behavior and
sudden bouts of irritability were enough to give them a sense that
something was off.

What's wrong with you? If they weren't saying it, which they
were with increasing frequency, then they were most definitely
thinking it.

By the time I got to the rock star's house I was desperate to get
high. We paid Billy, who waited in the driveway, and set out to
divide our take. The rock star immediately began to grind up five
or six pills, using a marble mortar and pestle. He cut four chalky
lines on the living-room coffee table with the edge of a small note-
pad and handed me a straw, which had been cut down to the
length of a cigarette. I leaned over, placed the straw in my right
nostril with my right hand, pinching the left nostril closed with
the knuckle of my left forefinger, and inhaled deeply.

"Why don't you hang out?" the rock star said. We sent Billy on his
way and got busy crushing and snorting our way through the night.

The higher we got, the more questions I asked. It was more of
an interview than a conversation.

"So tell me about groupies," I said as we both sat on the plush
white sofa, our feet up on the oversize glass coffee table.

"Who's the biggest asshole in the band?" I asked after we had
each snorted a couple more lines.

"Did you ever hook up with Naomi Campbell?" I inquired, sitting on the marble island in his giant kitchen watching as he made us smoothies.

And he went there. He talked. He trusted me.

I still felt high when I woke up the next day. I lay in the bed in the rock star's guesthouse, struggling to open my eyes. I could barely move my body, as if I was up to my neck in quicksand. It must have been late morning. The sun was pouring in through the floor-to-ceiling windows that made up one of the walls of the room. There was a framed platinum record leaning against the opposite wall just beneath a giant Peter Beard photograph of a lion, the edges covered with dried blood. I finally managed to swing my legs off the bed and sit myself up. I rubbed my hands over my eyes and looked out the window at the tennis court.

"So wait a minute," I said a few minutes later, drinking a Diet Coke from the can and standing next to the rock star on the back deck of the main house, "you play tennis?"

"Why is that so hard to believe?" he said. "I'm in great fucking shape. You think going out on tour is easy? At this age? No fucking way."

The rock star dressed like a rock star even when he was just bumming around the house. He was wearing tight black jeans torn at the knee, a pair of beat-up ankle-high black leather boots with faded rivets across the toe, and a vintage Gibson guitar T-shirt with a black collarless chambray shirt hanging open over the top.

"Let me ask you a question," he said. "Can you pay for the pills next time?"

"Um, okay," I stammered.

"Look, I don't have access to a lot of cash," he explained. "I have ex-wives and accountants and managers who all watch me like a hawk, man. No one can know I'm partying, and one of the ways they try to make sure I'm not is by limiting my access to cash."

"I got it," I said. "No problem."

"I can pay it back slowly or I can give you a signed guitar or some shit like that," he said.

"Say no more," I said. "I got you."

I understood what was at stake. What is was like to hide. How hard he must have been struggling to appear normal. He was running a con, just as I was.

I paid for the rock star's drugs regularly for the next year. We hung out a few more times, but things were getting serious with Sarah, and after we got engaged, I became more desperate than ever to finally stop. I saw Dr. Ron at least once a month, but I just couldn't stop. I saw Billy just as often.

Ten days before I flew to Australia for my wedding in 2005, I stopped taking opiates. It was the longest I'd gone without pills in five years. I toughed it out, with the help of Dr. Ron's shots and sheer willpower. I was white-knuckling it, but I just couldn't be high when I got married. I couldn't do that to Sarah. Or my family, for that matter, who all came to New York for the engagement party that David Copperfield hosted for us on the roof of his penthouse, and were about to fly to the other side of the world for our wedding.

The rock star called me a few days before I was scheduled to fly to Los Angeles, where I'd planned to stay for a night before heading off to Sydney, where Sarah had already been for a week putting the finishing touches on our reception.

"I'm clean right now," I told him when he asked if I wanted to call Billy and share a bottle of pills with him. "I feel pretty good and I don't want to fuck with that."

"That's awesome, man," he said. "Is there any chance I can borrow $1,500? I won't ask again, but I'm in a jam."

I wanted to say no, but I liked being friends with him. I didn't want to let him down.

"Sure thing," I said. "I'll be staying at the Beverly Hills Hotel. I'll leave it for you at the front desk."

Maybe it wasn't really a friendship, after all. Maybe we were just using each other. I got him high and kept his secret and he brought me into his orbit. Having celebrity friends had become its own kind of drug for me. It made me feel like an insider. That was worth $1,500 to me.

I left him the money, as promised, and boarded a Qantas flight to Sydney feeling a little nauseated from the opiate detox, but I didn't let it bother me. I had finally beaten the addiction. I was ready to start a new life with an incredible woman. A new beginning at last.

My sense of triumph wouldn't last long. It was the beginning, all right—the beginning of the end.

BUSTED

THEY DIDN'T KNOW MY NAME this time.

Maybe the doormen were new. It was hard to tell. They looked the same, with their comic book superhero jawlines and perfectly maintained three-day stubble, but New York City was loaded with guys like this—guys waiting to be discovered while working shift jobs behind the bar at trendy downtown lounges or modeling for midrange fashion catalogues or swinging the door open for guests at one of the city's many small boutique hotels.

Either way, they didn't know me. There was no "Welcome back, Mr. Peres!" this time. I was just another guy—as indistinguishable to them as they were to me—walking into the Morgans Hotel on that warm September afternoon in 2007. I carried a small, hastily packed brown leather Louis Vuitton duffel bag. I didn't have a reservation, but I needed a room.

My wife had thrown me out of the house.

I got the last available room in the hotel, a small dark one on the second floor, barely large enough to fit a queen-size bed, a desk, and a dresser. The room's only window looked out onto a narrow shaft and a brick wall about an arm's length away. I lay down on the bed, shoes on, and cried.

An hour earlier, I had been sitting in the living room of our large three-bedroom apartment on the sixty-first floor of a midtown high-rise, about to get high—without a care in the world. Large windows facing west offered stunning views to the Hudson River. Sarah was on her way to rehearsal in the Theater District ten blocks away for a play she was starring in about Frida Kahlo and Dorothy Hale. She played Kahlo's friend and benefactor, Clare Boothe Luce, and though Sarah was six months pregnant at the time, the costume designer had done an amazing job of concealing the baby bump.

I wasn't supposed to be there. It was early afternoon on a Thursday and I should have been at the office, which is where I'd told Sarah I was when we spoke shortly before I got back to the apartment. But I wasn't at work. I was waiting for her to leave home, watching the front door of our building from inside the small overpriced croissant and coffee place across the street. I watched, like a shady operative in a Cold War thriller, as she greeted the doorman on her way out, making her way down 56th Street and disappearing from view as she turned the corner to head down Seventh Avenue. I dashed across the street and went inside.

"You just missed your wife," the doorman said as I rushed into the building.

"Oh, man," I said. "I was hoping to see her before she left."

Once inside, I sat on the cream-colored sofa and counted out pills on the coffee table. The room had windows on three sides and was flooded with light. I had just swallowed seven 15-milligram Roxies when Sarah, having just arrived at the theater, called me and changed my life forever.

The apartment was beautiful. We had found it about eight months earlier after a long search. Sarah kept her house in LA, where we tried to spend as much time as we could, but she'd officially moved to New York. This was our first home as a couple, and we brought in an interior designer to help bring it to life. I was spending more time there than I should have been, some days not going into the office at all, making excuses to my staff about kidney disease and blood disorders and exhaustion. On these days, I would call in to the office, pretending to be in a doctor's office or sick in bed, and answer questions from the editors about which stories I wanted in the upcoming issue or which celebrity we should be trying to book for the cover. The fax machine was constantly humming as it churned out article after article waiting for my approval. Half the time I didn't even read them. I just lay in bed, high, and watched MTV, which seemed to be showing Rihanna's "Umbrella" video on a continuous loop, before nodding off. This was easier before the pregnancy, when Sarah was still spending a ton of time in LA working. When we were both in New York, together all of the time, the addiction got harder to conceal—the lies more frequent and elaborate and unbelievable.

The marriage didn't start out this way. There were no lies—at least for a couple of days. I managed to stay sober until our honeymoon, or what passed as a honeymoon. It was really more of a long weekend at a luxury resort in Cabo. We'd rented a small villa that had its own pool. From the moment we landed in Mexico, I planned to get drugs. But Cabo wasn't like Tijuana. There weren't three pharmacies on every block. I couldn't just casually slip out while she was in the shower and score the pills that I so desperately needed. I'd been hanging on by a thread in Australia, the only thing keeping me going the promise of drugs in Mexico.

I needed time to explore. Time to venture away from the resort and find not only a pharmacy but the right pharmacy.

"I just got off the phone with the office," I told Sarah after she woke from a nap. "I hate to do this, but I need to go to a local printing office and look at a high-resolution printout of our next cover. A faxed version won't do. My assistant found a place about twenty minutes away. I promise I won't be gone for more than an hour."

I jumped in a cab and told the driver to take me to the closest pharmacy. It wasn't until we went to the fourth one, miles away from the beach and the swanky hotels that I found what I was looking for—four small white boxes of Tylenol with Codeine. With the wild abandon of a kid opening a present on Christmas morning, I tore into a box in the back seat of the taxi and swallowed a whole sleeve of pills, twelve in all, one at a time without water. It had been two weeks since my last high.

The honeymoon was over.

The first year of my marriage was one long series of stops and starts. Sarah had been asking, "What's wrong with you?" on a weekly basis and on more than one occasion had asked me point-blank if I was using drugs again. "Of course not," I'd say. But the signs must have been clear. I couldn't get out of bed in the morning, and when I went to office—if I went at all—I would be back at home a few hours later.

"I need to read all of these pages," I'd say by way of explanation. "I can't get it done in the office. Too many interruptions."

I'd close myself off in the bedroom that we'd converted into a home office and drift off into a drug-induced stupor while pretending to read. Even Dr. Ron was getting concerned. His usual Zen-like demeanor had been replaced by a firmness that I didn't even know he was capable of.

"You need to go to rehab, Dan," he said. "You're coming in here now every two weeks. You can't keep this up."

"I want to stop," I told him, tears in my eyes. "I really do. I just can't."

"I can see that," he said, "but I'm beginning to think that I can't help you. You need to be in an inpatient facility. You need meetings and structure, Dan. You need to be around people who can give you the tools of recovery."

I didn't want to be around people. I could barely bring myself to look at anyone. I would walk out of our apartment building some mornings, using all the energy I had to push the revolving door, and just stand on the sidewalk gazing at the swarm of New Yorkers breezing past me.

How do they do it? I'd think. *How do they keep going?*

I envied everyone. Especially Sarah. The way she'd wake early and jump into her day, running to auditions and seeing friends. Smiling and healthy. I never wanted to do anything.

"It's beautiful out," she'd say. "Let's go to the park."

"What?" I said. "I'm not going to the park and sitting around with a bunch of tourists in shorts. That's not what real New Yorkers do, Sarah. Come on, cut it out. I have work to do."

Most of the time, envy would quickly turn to resentment, and I would lash out, sometimes viciously. At Sarah. At my staff. At my mom. Anyone—even strangers.

Like, for example, the night when Sarah and I were having dinner at Seppi's, a crowded French bistro across the street and down the block from our apartment. When I did agree to go out and do something "normal," I did it on my own terms and not readily. "Fine," I'd say, "but I want to go somewhere close. I'm not going downtown."

The restaurant was packed, the air heavy with the smell of garlic and fresh-baked bread.

"Can you believe this place?" I said. "No one's even come to give us menus yet. We had to go out, didn't we? I'm not leaving a tip, I'll tell you that."

We hadn't been there for more than five minutes.

The booth we were in backed up to a narrow walkway next to the wooden podium where the hostess stood. People waiting for tables were congregating right behind me, and someone must have accidently bumped the back of the booth I was sitting in. It wasn't bolted to the floor and it moved. Without even thinking, I aggressively bucked backward, sliding the booth into the walkway and knocking into the couple standing behind me.

"What's wrong with you?" a man in his mid-thirties asked. "You just hit my wife."

"You just shoved me into the table," I said, turning around to look at him and his wife. She was pregnant.

"It was an accident," he said. "Take it easy."

"Well, I didn't hear you apologize," I said. Sarah was understandably mortified.

"Sorry," he said. "But you don't have to behave that way. You can act like a human at least."

I was trying to, but it was proving impossible. The only thing I cared about was drugs. My unrelenting need for them had long ago transcended the bounds of acceptable human behavior.

It's also quite possible that my drug use was preventing Sarah from getting pregnant. After trying for six months, we went to see one of New York's preeminent fertility specialists and began IVF treatments. I tried to stop again, fully aware that all of the injections and poking and prodding that Sarah was having to endure might well have been because of me. The day before we were scheduled for our first IVF procedure, I threw a full bottle of Roxicodone down the garbage chute in our apartment building. I was done. I simply couldn't bear to think about what I was putting her through. But I didn't even make it till the next morning. I went down to the lobby after midnight, once Sarah was asleep, and explained to the doorman that I'd accidently thrown away my medication. He called the building's overnight porter, who took me to the trash room in the subbasement.

"I don't know if you really want to go through this mess," he said, "but you're welcome to. We bagged and took out the trash last night, so what's here is from today."

Wearing a pair of plaid pajama pants, a T-shirt, and flip-flops, I climbed into a large plastic bin the size of a compact car and began digging through mounds of trash. The porter just stood there watching. After ten minutes, I found the pill bottle. I went upstairs, rinsed it off, and got high.

Once Sarah was pregnant, my use escalated. And so did her suspicions. I'd always loved children. From the time I was a little boy, I loved playing with other people's children—showing them magic tricks and juggling for them. I couldn't wait to be a father. But I was terrified. I knew I needed to stop before our baby was born, but I couldn't.

Dr. Ron wasn't treating me anymore. He refused, unless I'd agreed to go away to rehab. The closer we got to Sarah's due date, the more anxious I became and the more I used. I was taking more pills than I'd ever taken. I was waking up in the middle of the night to get high. I was FedExing cash to Billy and having him send me pills. And of course I was still seeing the two pain specialists who hadn't yet caught on the way Donna and Dr. Fine had.

I was getting careless. Over the last few months, Sarah had begun spotting charges at various pharmacies on our credit card statements. I usually ran the prescriptions through insurance when I could and paid for the rest of them with cash, but since I'd sent Billy $1,500 a couple of times, I had no choice but to charge them. The first time Sarah asked about a several-hundred-dollar credit card charge, I made up a lie about needing some things for a shoot on grooming products that we were doing at the magazine.

I tried serving up the same lie the second time she asked, the day I watched her leave for rehearsal. She had just gotten off the phone with our accountant, whom she'd asked to review our credit card bills for charges at pharmacies, when she called me. Our accountant had confirmed her suspicions.

"I don't believe you," she said. "You're doing drugs. I know you are."

"What are you talking about?" I said. "You know that I have to charge things for work on my personal card sometimes."

"You're lying to me," she said.

I sat on our living-room sofa, the pills that I swallowed a few minutes earlier starting to make their way into my bloodstream, trying to figure a way out of the situation. I had been manufacturing lies for so long, and they usually came quickly, but nothing was coming this time.

"You're taking drugs again, aren't you?" she said. "Just tell me the truth."

"I am," I said.

It was over. She'd been through enough and I'd had enough.

"I'm pregnant," she said. "I'm about to have our baby. I don't want you at the apartment when I get home. How could you do this? What's wrong with you?"

What's wrong with you?

I was finally asking myself the same question.

I WAS LYING on the bed at the Morgans when Adam called.

"Where are you?" he asked.

"I'm at work. I can't talk," I said.

"Bullshit," he said. "Sarah called me and told me what's going on. Where the fuck are you?"

"The Morgans Hotel," I said.

"I'll be right there."

When Adam showed up thirty minutes later, I burst into tears.

"Do you have any pills?" he asked.

"Yes," I said. "And I'm high right now."

"Give me the pills," he said.

Adam took the bottle of Roxicodone that I'd tossed in my bag with a change of clothes and my Dopp kit before leaving the apartment and dumped them into the toilet.

"You're done, brother," he said. "Enough."

"I know," I said, crying. "I want to be done. I'm so fucking relieved that she knows. That you know."

"Your family knows, too," Adam said. "Sarah told them. I spoke with your mom on the way over here. You've got to see this for what it is. It's a wake-up call. You're about to be a father. It's time to start acting like it."

"I know," I said. "I want it over with."

"You want what over with?" he said. "I don't need to take your shoelaces and belt or anything like that, do I?"

"No," I said. "I want to be done with this. With the pills."

Adam spent the night with me at the Morgans and waited with me the following morning until my father and brother, who were driving up from Baltimore, arrived to take me back home with them.

I laid down in the back seat of my dad's car and didn't say a word. I tried to sleep, but I couldn't. When we got to my mother's house we sat down, as a family. They asked me if I wanted to go to rehab and told me that they'd already researched it.

"No," I said. "I just want to stay here. I want to go through the detox here. I've done it before. I did it right before the wedding. Let me just stay here."

My mom and my brother took my bag and dumped it out on the kitchen table. They started going through my things, searching for drugs.

"Adam already took them," I said.

"Well, we're going to double-check," my brother said.

They took out each article of clothing and pulled at it and shook it and examined it, like prison guards searching for a hidden shank. Something fell from the pocket of my khakis and bounced onto the table in front of them.

"Get it," my mom told my brother. "Flush it."

My brother grabbed a round pink object and ran to the bathroom and threw it in the toilet. "Gone," he said.

"That was an Altoid," I told them. "A cinnamon Altoid. Nice work."

Going from upward of sixty pills a day to none is a bit like driving 100 miles an hour and slamming on the brakes. You're all over the place and not exactly sure what's going to happen. Doing it in your Jewish mother's house is even more intense.

My mother worried about me even when she thought everything was fine. This was intense. Every time I'd get out of bed to go to the bathroom, which was often, she called upstairs to me: "Are you okay?" And every time she'd hear the toilet flush, she'd call upstairs, "Good boy. Get the junk out of your body."

I stayed there for two weeks, speaking with Sarah only once, though my mother talked to her several times a day. Nights were the worst. I couldn't get comfortable and my entire body was restless.

In the middle of all of this, I had to deal with a crisis at the magazine. I'd told my staff and my boss that I was down in Baltimore dealing with a back problem and that I needed to take some time to recover. But this couldn't wait. We had recently put Ben Affleck on the cover of *Details*, and he was furious over some things that were written in the story that shouldn't have made it past our fact-checker. I had to get on the phone with him and assure him that we were taking this seriously and were planning an unprecedented correction. So there I was, sitting in the den of my mother's house, a shivering, quivering mess with a blanket wrapped around me, talking to Ben Affleck.

"I accept full responsibility for what's happened here," I told him. "And I am sorry for putting you through this."

I may have been speaking to him, but I was really talking to everyone—Sarah, my family, the staff at *Details*. Sarah, while grateful that I was going through detox, wasn't ready to have me back in the apartment.

"Just give her time," my mom told me. "You've put her through a lot."

I needed to go back to New York and get back to work. I was scheduled to begin an intensive outpatient program at a facility just off Madison Avenue, which had been recommended by my shrink.

"Can you call one of your friends and maybe stay on their sofa for a few nights?" my mother asked.

So I turned to the person who had always been there for me. I called David Copperfield.

"Hey there," I said when he answered his cell phone. "It's Dan. Listen, David . . . um, I'm a drug addict. I'm in Baltimore getting sober."

"Is there anything I can do to help?" he said.

"I'm coming back to New York in a couple of days," I explained. "Sarah isn't ready for me to come home yet—understandably. Would it be possible for me to stay at your apartment for a few nights?"

"Stay as long as you need," he said.

MAGIC

THERE ARE NO BAD HIGHS.

Not to me, anyway. Not with painkillers. Some highs are better than others, but in the end, like with pizza or sex, even the ones that underdeliver . . . deliver.

There are, however, many different types of high.

There's the hotel-room high. The Sunday-afternoon high. The early-morning-get-back-in-bed high. The nobody-can-know-I'm-high high.

There's the I-think-I'm-going-to-die high. The I-have-no-more-pills-left high. And of course, the I'm-never-getting-high-again-after-this-time high. There were a lot of those.

After a brutal fourteen-day detox at my mother's tidy, *Elle Decor*–inspired house in Baltimore, I was finally heading back to New York. Anxious, I took my seat on the train and waited. Reality was creeping in as slowly and steadily as the southbound Metroliner on the opposite track. I wasn't ready for what awaited me at home—a heartbroken and angry wife who'd been lied to from day one, a bewildered and leaderless staff at the magazine, and an outpatient drug program that I'd already regretted agreeing to attend.

The only thing I was truly looking forward to was the I-haven't-been-high-in-two-weeks high that was waiting for me in Manhattan.

"GETTING CLEAN IS the easy part. Staying clean takes work," the sixty-something man with the mustache told me. "It's not going to happen until you're ready. Addiction doesn't just go away."

This I knew.

I'd wished it away for years. Begged Dr. Ron to take it away. Prayed to a god that I wasn't sure I believed in to make it disappear as effortlessly as a simple coin vanish.

No luck.

It didn't work that way. I'd learned this the hard way. I didn't need to hear it from the man with the mustache. I knew you couldn't just hide from addiction under the covers at your mom's house as if avoiding the school bully, that you couldn't just puke it up or flush it down or sweat it out.

This wasn't the flu or a zit—where you could lay low and ride it out for a week until it's gone. There's no chicken soup or Clearasil for addiction.

I knew all of this. I was obviously still missing something—the elusive secret code that would help me solve the puzzle—like an ancient keystone in a Dan Brown novel—and finally fix me. This is what I wanted from the guy with the mustache at the AA meeting. I was seeking wisdom, not that "one day at a time" bullshit.

For as long as I can remember, I'd been searching for a short-cut. I'd never been terribly interested in putting in the work. If there was a test at school, I was cramming for it on the bus that morning. I read CliffsNotes instead of books and hastily slapped together projects the night before that other kids had been working on for weeks.

"If Danny applied himself more, he would be an exceptional student." My mom and dad must have heard this at dozens of parent/teacher conferences over the years. But I didn't need to work any harder than I already was. Cutting corners got me into NYU and sent to Paris and the job at *Details* by age twenty-seven. If there was a shortcut, I was taking it. So that's what I was hoping to find when one of my mother's oldest friends, Lou, took me to an AA meeting while I was detoxing in Baltimore.

I'd known Lou my entire life. Her real name was Louise, but my brother and I had been calling her Aunt Lou our whole lives. When I was growing up, Aunt Lou was always at our house. I remember her sitting at the white kitchen table smoking Merit Ultra Light cigarettes with my mom when I was a young boy and moms still sat around kitchen tables smoking. Aside from the cigarettes, which Aunt Lou gave up the same day as my mom in the late eighties, she was a health nut. She did aerobics every day when that was still a thing, before becoming an early suburban devotee of yoga.

Aunt Lou was reed-thin, had a year-round tan, and always brought me Twizzlers when she visited, which was often. She was like family, but I wasn't up for seeing her when my mother told me she wanted to come by.

"I think you should talk to her," my mother said. "She's coming over tonight."

"Mom, look at me. I'm a mess. It's enough that you're seeing me this way, I don't need your friends rolling through here like it's some kind of petting zoo," I said.

"Listen to me, sweetie," my mom said. "You need to trust me and see your aunt Lou."

I couldn't really fight her. I didn't have the energy. I hadn't slept more than a few hours in my first five days in Baltimore. I had the second floor of my mom's beautifully appointed two-story white brick house all to myself. There were two large bedrooms, a small office, and a bathroom. Restless, I paced the tan carpeted hallway in the middle of the night—down and back like the Queen's Guard—my mother occasionally coming out from her bedroom directly below to see if I was okay.

Nights were the worst. I tried sleeping in both of the bedrooms, spending an hour or so in one bed before moving to the other, desperate for a reprieve. I had uncontrollable chills, which wasn't helped by the fact that my mother loved to keep her house very cool, particularly at night. It was like a cryo chamber in there. I was freezing one second and drenched in sweat the next. I took two, sometimes three, showers a night—shivering under the hot water, hoping to somehow rinse off the addiction like salt after a swim in the ocean.

There was a white bookshelf directly across from the bathroom. Every night when I got out of the shower, I stood weak and naked in the bathroom doorway, a white bath towel draped over my shoulders, and stared blankly at the framed family photos on the shelves in front of me. There I was, celebrating weddings and bar mitzvahs; at summer camp and graduating from college. I wasn't smiling in any of the pictures.

The nights were long.

I was thirty-five years old and my mother was still taking care of me. Despite all of her stereotypical Jewish-mom-ness, my mother rose to the occasion with extraordinary composure and a level of measured calm I don't remember ever seeing before. Both she and Sarah saved my life. Sarah for having the courage to throw me out and the wisdom to sound an alarm. And my mom for having the strength to watch her youngest son fall apart right in front of her eyes and the grace to calmly pick up the pieces.

But in the end, she was also a stereotypical Jewish mom and she ran a rehab the way one might expect a Jewish mother would—she fed me.

"You need to eat something," she said. "Get your strength back."

The kitchen counter was lined with bottles of Pepto-Bismol and Imodium and Tylenol and ginger ale. She served up chicken broth and turkey sandwiches on thick slices of challah. I went from having no appetite to eating everything in sight. I lost five pounds the first week I was there and gained ten the second. I was sitting at the kitchen table eating my second grilled-cheese sandwich when Aunt Lou walked in.

She sat down next to me in my mom's kitchen. She had a pack of Twizzlers in her hand.

"I don't think you know this, but I'm an alcoholic," she said matter-of-factly. "I've been sober for seven years."

She told me that she used to drink a bottle of wine a day by herself and then hide the bottles in the garage where no one would find them.

"But you've always been so healthy," I said. "All the yoga and stuff."

"That was my cover, darling," she said, taking my hand. "Don't get me wrong, I love exercising, but I always figured that no one would suspect I had a problem if they saw me working out all of the time. I didn't want anyone asking me any questions about my drinking."

Aunt Lou explained that she went to AA meetings almost every day and told me there was one starting in forty-five minutes just a short drive from my mom's house.

"Do you want to come with me?" she asked.

"But I'm a drug addict, not an alcoholic," I said.

"It's all the same, angel," she said. "Trust me."

Aunt Lou drove me down the long winding driveway to the campus of Sheppard Pratt. I'd never been there before but knew it was a mental hospital. I'd always pictured *One Flew Over the Cuckoo's Nest* whenever I drove past—crazy people in hospital gowns flinging applesauce at each other and fighting over crayons.

There were half a dozen people standing outside of a small building smoking cigarettes and laughing. I couldn't imagine what anyone going to an AA meeting had to laugh about, and I looked at them curiously as Aunt Lou led me into the building. I was terrified. Inside, there were folding chairs set up in a U-shape around a small table where the man with the mustache was sitting.

"You're in the right place," he said warmly after Aunt Lou introduced us.

The meeting wasn't what I was expecting, even though I had no idea what to expect. The people were clean and well dressed. Young and old. And there wasn't a trench coat in sight. I don't know why, but I was expecting men in trench coats. Halfway through the meeting, the man with the mustache, who seemed to be running things, asked if anyone was celebrating an anniversary. A young, healthy-looking guy in jeans and a polo shirt, who couldn't have been more than twenty-five, stood up and said that it had been six months since he'd last done drugs. I was floored. I looked at him in awe. *How on earth did he manage that?* I thought.

I sat perfectly still in my chair, listening as people shared their stories. I was just starting to relax when an older man standing in the back of the room raised his hand and started to speak.

"I was sober for twenty-seven years," he said, his voice trembling as he spoke. "I was on a plane last week and the stewardess asked me if I wanted a drink and I said yes. Just like that. I drank three vodkas by the time we landed."

What the fuck? I was shocked, but everyone around me just listened and nodded their heads.

"I'll tell you this," he continued. "It'll sneak up on you if you're not careful."

"How can that happen?" I asked Aunt Lou as we were driving home. "How could that guy just order a drink on that plane?"

"It happens," she said. "It happens all the time. Do you know how much courage it took for him to walk in that room and tell on himself like that?"

"Wow, that's amazing," I said.

"You need to tell on yourself, too," she said. "You need to call the doctors you were getting the pills from and tell them you are an addict."

"I know," I said. "I will."

"Good," said Aunt Lou, pulling her large black BMW into my mom's driveway. "I'll be over in the morning and we can do it together."

I knew the phone numbers by heart. I was ready to tell on myself. Aunt Lou showed up a little after ten A.M. I was going back to New York the next day, and this needed to happen. My first call was to Donna in Dr. Fine's office. I was nervous.

"Hi, Donna. It's Dan Peres. I'm a drug addict," I said.

She couldn't have been sweeter and asked if there was anything that she and Stanley could do for me. I explained that I'd spent the last two weeks detoxing and that my parents had registered me in an outpatient rehab program.

"We're here for you if you need us, Dan," she told me.

The next call was to Dr. Leo Krauss. His receptionist, Nikki, whom I knew well, told me that he was with a patient and asked if the doctor could call me back.

"It's urgent," I told her. "I just need to speak with him now for a minute."

Dr. Krauss always wore three-piece suits and we often discussed bespoke tailoring when I was in his examining room. Like Donna, he wasn't surprised and was pleased to know I was getting help.

I had planned to make one more call that morning, to Dr. Scott Shaw. Aunt Lou looked at me proudly as I held the phone. I put it down on the kitchen table and smiled.

"That's it," I said. "Wow, that felt great."

In that instant, I had decided to keep using. It was as simple as that. Like the man in the meeting who ordered a drink on the plane, it just happened. I didn't even think about it. Using drugs had become my default. My escape. It had been my go-to for seven years. It's what I did.

I was visiting an older friend once a few years earlier, and his teenage son was sitting in the living room doing math homework. While I was waiting for his dad to get ready to go out to dinner, the son was going on and on about his love of fractions.

"There are infinite divisions between 0 and 1," he said. "You could literally spend forever fractioning between the two numbers. If it was the distance of an inch, most of the fractions would be imperceptible to the human eye. But they exist nonetheless. There's a ton of stuff going on between 0 and 1, you know?"

A lot can happen in one second. That's precisely how long it took me to decide I wasn't done.

I was somewhere between Wilmington and Philadelphia when I called Dr. Shaw's office from the train. Every now and then, he would let me come by to pick up my Roxicodone prescription without an examination. I asked Anna, the receptionist, if the doctor would leave it for me at the front desk.

"It's here waiting for you," she told me after a brief hold. "I'm running out to pick up lunch in a few minutes. Do you want me to drop it at the pharmacy downstairs?"

"Perfect," I said. "Thanks, Anna."

I went right from Penn Station to the pharmacy, paying for the pills with the $200 that my father had given me so I could have some money in my pocket when I went home.

I had arranged with Sarah for me to come by the apartment and get some clothes before going to Copperfield's apartment. We'd spoken only once while I was in Baltimore. She wasn't there when I got home and I quickly packed a bag and made my way to David's, the prescription bottle tucked into the front pocket of my jeans.

David was mainly living in Las Vegas, where he performed twice every night at the MGM Grand. He'd arranged for one of his assistants to meet me at the apartment building to introduce me to the doormen and help me get settled. It was close to five P.M. when I finally took the pills. I sat on the edge of the bed in the guest room and swallowed seven 15-milligram Roxies with a small bottle of Fiji Water I took from the kitchen and gazed out the floor-to-ceiling windows at the city below.

The high rushed over me like a giant wave. It was intense. I hadn't had any opiates in my system for two weeks and probably should have taken fewer pills. When I lay down, it felt like I was sinking into the bed. I couldn't move. And I didn't, for the rest of the night.

The first thing I saw the following morning was the pill bottle on the nightstand. I lay there, still wearing my clothes and shoes, and stared at it.

Take 1–2 tablets by mouth every 4–6 hours as needed for pain.

I was three months away from becoming a father and I had gotten so high the night before I couldn't even take my shoes off.

"Getting clean is the easy part," I remembered the man with the mustache telling me a few nights earlier. "Staying clean takes work."

"Time to do the work," I said out loud to myself and got out of bed and flushed the pills down the toilet.

I was ready.

I stayed at David's apartment for over a month, going to AA meetings every day, sometimes twice a day. Sarah eventually agreed to let me come home.

Oscar Peres was born on a bitterly cold January morning in 2008. I had been sober for ninety-two days. Late that night, as Sarah slept in the hospital room, I pushed Oscar around the maternity ward in a clear basinet on wheels. He was wrapped tightly in a blanket and had a tiny cotton cap on his head. All I could see was his chubby red face. He lay there staring up at me as I walked.

"All right, buddy," I said, looking into his eyes. "We're both kind of new to this world. Let's figure it out together."

I looked up and saw a woman in a white robe pushing her own newborn toward me. I smiled and congratulated her. She stopped to look at Oscar.

"Isn't it just the most amazing thing in the world?" she said. "It kind of makes you believe in magic, doesn't it?"

"It sure does," I said.

Acknowledgments

THIS BOOK WOULD HAVE BEEN impossible to write without the love and support of my family and friends. Lisa and Jerry Sopher, Ed Peres, and Jeff Peres—I am still here today and able to tell this story because of you. I am more grateful than I can say to have you in my corner.

Thank you to Aviva Wolf, the best non-editor editor I've ever seen, who pushed me and kept me honest and always told me the truth. None of this would have happened without you.

Tons of gratitude to my agent and friend, Bill Clegg, for believing in this book long before I sat down to write it. And special thanks to everyone at the Clegg Agency, notably Simon Toop, David Kambhu, Lilly Sandberg, Marion Duvert, and Kristen Wolf, for your help and support.

A huge thank you to my amazing editor, Sara Nelson, and the team at HarperCollins—Mary Gaule, Tom Hopke, Emily Van-Derwerken, Robin Bilardello, and Jonathan Burnham.

Thank you to those generous and brilliant friends who read and reread and then read some more along the way. I owe an impossible-to-repay debt to the extraordinary DeLauné Michel, who took the time to respond to every email, text, and call, and who talked me off of the ledge on a daily basis. Jeff Berman, Jeff Gordinier, and Andrew Essex—thank you for helping shape this story. And massive thanks go to Luke Dempsey, who lit the fire and gave me great guidance.

About the Author

DAN PERES was editor in chief of *Details* for fifteen years, starting in 2000, when the title relaunched under his leadership. During his tenure, the magazine won many awards, including two National Magazine Awards. Before taking the editorship of *Details*, Dan spent nine years at *W* magazine, overseeing bureaus in Paris, London, and Milan. While in college, he worked as a copy boy at the *New York Times* and later as a research assistant at *Esquire*. He is the author of *Details Men's Style Manual*. He lives in New York and has three sons.